Star Man

Star Man

♦

Regaining Your Life's Balance

Gary Combs

iUniverse, Inc.
New York Lincoln Shanghai

Star Man
Regaining Your Life's Balance

Copyright © 2007 by Gary W. Combs

All rights reserved. No part of this book may be used or reproduced by any means, graphic, electronic, or mechanical, including photocopying, recording, taping or by any information storage retrieval system without the written permission of the publisher except in the case of brief quotations embodied in critical articles and reviews.

iUniverse books may be ordered through booksellers or by contacting:

iUniverse
2021 Pine Lake Road, Suite 100
Lincoln, NE 68512
www.iuniverse.com
1-800-Authors (1-800-288-4677)

The views expressed in this work are solely those of the author and do not necessarily reflect the views of the publisher, and the publisher hereby disclaims any responsibility for them. Biblical references throughout this book are based on the Zondervan NIV Study Bible (Fully Revised), Copyright 1985, 1995, 2002. Published by The Zondervan Corporation, Grand Rapids, Michigan, 49530, U.S.A.

ISBN-13: 978-0-595-41291-4 (pbk)
ISBN-13: 978-0-595-85647-3 (ebk)
ISBN-10: 0-595-41291-2 (pbk)
ISBN-10: 0-595-85647-0 (ebk)

Printed in the United States of America

Dedicated to Stephanie, Jamie
and Jackson Combs

Contents

My Sincere Thanks and Gratitude ix

Preface xi

Introduction 1

Love 11

Family 19

Work 27

Community 40

Health 46

God 57

Epilogue 85

How To Recognize A Star Man 87

Food For Thought and Discussion 89

Notes 93

APPENDIX 95

Suggested Further Reading For Men 97

About the Author 99

My Sincere Thanks and Gratitude

Over the course of the past ten years, I have been blessed by associates, friends, and family, all of whom have contributed to this undertaking. While they may be unaware, our conversations and activities have brought about many of the personal stories which have been shared here. My brothers, Mark and Craig, have always served as a constant source of strength; they have often helped me stay "centered" when it seemed things were going haywire. My father, Clarence, has never failed to share his reasoned perspective on whatever topics we discussed. Quite often, he would say a great deal by saying nothing at all. Silence can be deafening. His influence can be traced throughout these pages.

I have been privileged to know several high-quality men in the context of social life, service within the church, business, or community involvement. They have contributed to this work in more ways than I can adequately convey. I would like several very special men to know how grateful I am: Don Douglas, Floyd Gilbert, Ralph O'Connell, Clint Damuth, and John Ritzo.

Without having told him so, I appreciate the time shared and insights gained from the times I have spent with Dr. Tom Currie, author of *Searching For Truth: Confessing Christ In An Uncertain World*, and author of *Ambushed By Grace—The Virtues Of A Useless Faith*. He personifies the attributes of calm demeanor and quiet strength which many men could only aspire to. He helped motivate me to return to my writing which may otherwise have lain dormant.

Many thanks also go to Linda Cobb, my relatively new friend and fellow church member, who has shared her gifts of speech, writing, and editing. The ideas expressed in these words are clearer as a result of my following some writing fundamentals she has provided. Without her assistance, I am certain that these personalized messages to men would yield less impact or meaning. If the editing process has missed punctuation errors or inadequate phraseology, please know that they are the result of my capacity as a student rather than the skills presented by the teacher!

    Most of all, I am grateful to my daughters, Stephanie and Jamie, and to my wife, Joni. Over the past ten years, the girls have taken the time to read and respond to my personal notes to them. Their perspectives have been invaluable. To an even greater extent, my wife has put up with my continuous involvement outside the home. She has refrained from threatening me with bodily harm—at least so far—if I were to add any new activities to my schedule without prior consultation with her. Our relationship has strengthened and grown deeper beyond any that I could ever have imagined. I am blessed by the love she shows me every day.

Preface

Have you ever had a gut feeling that kept gnawing at you? Or, have you ever heard that quiet yet persistent voice inside saying, "Write these things down, and send them to the people you care about most?" For me, this constant bug started back in 1995. Maybe some day, when my daughters got a little older, they would be able to read some of my sporadic scribbling and get a better sense of just where I'm coming from as their Dad. I believe this to be especially true of the times leading up to and soon following my divorce from their mother.

Surprising myself, I actually began the process. It was Sunday evening, September 3rd, 1995. During the work week, I was able to be in my daughters' home area in eastern Pennsylvania for business and called my two daughters, as I often would, to see them that particular Thursday. Our time together began with dinner at Bertucci's, near a local mall, with my younger daughter. Our one-on-one feast was filled with conversation and often my laughter over how fast this bright young fourteen year old could talk. Later on, I was able to visit with my older daughter while she was working at the Sheraton health club and gym even though she was obviously very distracted or disturbed by my being there. I eventually came to understand—months later—that she had already become too grown up to have Dad around while she was working.

I remember thinking to myself how they were growing up so fast. I was afraid they would be educated, married, and moved away before I could blink. By this time in our lives, I was living nearly 300 miles away. While driving back home to Virginia Beach after our time together, I thought a lot about how many times I had already made that trip. As dads' minds often tend to wander, I saw a steady stream of flashbacks, mostly about how cute they looked during earlier days. Burned into my memory is the image of the girls going over to the beach from our condo for the local Labor Day weekend celebration. It was the annual Low Rent Regatta. With boogie boards in hand, beach towels slung over their shoulders, summer bronze tans that only the younger ones can get without any effort, sleepy-eyes, messy-hair, and smiling faces, these two were a picture of youthful exuberance. Tons of other flashbacks raced through my mind—some were of warm and loving memories and some were of painful times. Deep feelings of gloom would creep in every time I had to drop them off on a Sunday evening and drive the five hours back home. Frequent thoughts of some of the difficulties we were all experiencing during these times made those return trips seem very, very long.

On that particular weekend, I also managed to do some office clean-up and reorganization work. It was part of my wanting to be organized so I could work on a new position—a promotion to General Manager at my work place. For several years, I had not talked much with my girls about my work, the former small business that I owned, or my income. You see, with all that had been discussed or debated during the early years of divorce, I had became very guarded—even consciously reluctant—to say a word at all concerning such things. If you have ever had a similar experience or know someone who has, you can understand that sometimes you just keep these things to yourself. In my case, this was especially true of promotions, which, if publicized, would likely become fodder for an increase in child support. At the time, I was already providing much more than the court required.

So I learned to just keep silent on such subjects. Pity, too, because building my own business as a manufacturers' representative, taking on an honest and hardworking partner, and later selling out to him, were all very exciting personal moments. When I became president of a company in this same industry, I found it equally challenging, yet rewarding and gratifying. In fact, this newest promotion to general management was the "next high" for me and was becoming just as much fun and satisfying. But again, it wasn't something to be discussed with my children given the circumstances.

Now, that's about all the background you need in order to get a sense of what has motivated me to put together these words. But, to be perfectly clear, let me say only this:

My story is not unique. In numerous ways, I suggest that yours isn't all that different either. I promise that in so many of the pages you are about to read, you will back away from time to time and say to yourself, "Yep, it's a guy thing."

So, where is this going? What meaning does this have for you? Well, for starters, in this one snapshot you get the picture that sometimes things do not turn out as we had planned or hoped. Some really good things happen—plenty of joyful times. Yet, a number of heartaches dot a man's landscape as well. Through so many "life experiences," and usually in the tough times, we often question or doubt ourselves. A fairly common tool that guys use for sorting things out is to jot down personal notes immediately after any kind of troubling time. Somehow, seeing things on paper or even going back over them after some time had passed seemed to put them into a clearer perspective.

From such times, the fragmented memoirs I kept over several years had become dormant. It was on my return from that particular trip to see the girls that I found a lot of old notes. In truth, my attempt at a journal had always consisted of disjointed ramblings—sometimes even rants. Fun notes from family outings often made the pages of my theme book. It revealed several trips which we had planned but not actually taken. Scribbles in the margins gave hints at things I wanted to do the next time we were together. As I said, this spiral-ring notebook contained all sorts of odd notes dating back to when I had first moved out of our house in suburbia, post divorce. So, as a result of my reflections that weekend, it has long been on my mind to share with other guys, just like you, my thoughts, feelings, hardships, and joys. To the extent that men ever discuss real stuff, like feelings, consider this work to be *guy talk*.

What I believe you will find in these pages is not some carefully scripted road map for your personal success. You will find real experiences shared in straightforward language. Academic-types like to offer sophisticated discourses. In the same spirit as one of my early heroes, President Harry Truman, I want this to be filled with honest talk in plain English. You will not need a dictionary to understand what is written here. These are simply the views of an ordinary layman like yourself and hopefully a couple of thought-starters for you. It is meant to offer insight and to help you renew yourself, perhaps with the additional help of a close friend. If you already have some form of spiritual life or prayer life, now would be a good time to take a moment for silent reflection!

So, you say you are not accustomed to talking about *feelings* (that dreaded word among the male population), or you don't even like to think about such things? If so, you may never discover that you are not alone in such thoughts. Your experiences and times of personal adversity are something you and your buddies have in common. The real question is, "Are you willing to expose your concerns, your fears, or your prideful tendencies?" We men, in general, are not natural-born *sharers*. We can talk infinitely about all the good things in our lives. But what about our weaknesses, our dark side? Heck no! We can't let anybody see that. What would they think of us, right? But that is exactly the point we can get to.

If reading these words achieves anything for you, I would pray that it at least helps you see some of the life-changing nuggets that are the direct result of both *your* difficulties and *your* times of joy.

The final pages of this book contain my thumbnail biographical sketch. What it says is that I am the product of a middle-class American family, born in a small community west of Pittsburgh, Pennsylvania, and raised through high school in suburban Cincinnati. It is from the vantage point of these quite *average* circumstances that my most meaningful lessons have been drawn (and still seem to come beaming through from time to time). Let me also say that many of the experiences described in these chapters are my direct reflections on what happens *when values clash*—values that can be traced back to those simple, formative years. I would encourage you to watch for this recurring theme as you read.

Let me say from the outset, that I have another reason for this venture. I have been blessed. If I have done a work of this type any justice, it will shine a light on many crucial aspects of a man's upbringing, on things we see or don't see as boys, and on our peaks and valleys (our sources of growth and character development) through young adulthood and beyond.

In the back of the book, you will find a few questions or thought-starters for each of the key chapters. Either in private, or in the company of a friend or two, I encourage you to use them. It is my sincere hope that this book offers you new seeds for personal growth. I also hope it contributes to your finding balance in your own purposes and goals.

Introduction

It had long bothered me that my daughters and I had lost so much time together, especially when they were teenagers. They never got much of the kind of family upbringing that I had. Unfortunately, I can see that broken families are all too common.

Before I go on, let me attempt at least a thumbnail sketch of the most important parts of my own early years, which I understand and appreciate so much more now as an adult than when I was growing up. As you step into my picture from boyhood, I suggest you ask yourself this question, "What has my own experience been?"

My two brothers and I were surrounded by family—eighteen cousins if I'm adding correctly and lots of second cousins whom I surely couldn't name now. We were surrounded by lots of aunts and uncles and our grandparents; they were around all the time. Mother's side of the family was mostly within a five-mile area. Dad's side was only twenty-some miles away, yet it was still thought of as "going to the country" to see them. At home, the sense of closeness and supportive relationships among neighbors was the norm. Our church was small, but it was an extension of home which provided a real sense of being an integral part of my family. Everyone knew each other—not just names, but who they were, where they may have come from, and where they lived.

At family gatherings, we enjoyed singing while someone played piano, and we joined in with the frequent outbursts of laughter as certain participants' voices bore no resemblance to the tune that the rest were singing. When family conversations turned to serious things or conflicts, we youngsters sensed it. As kids, we were always watching the adults. We noticed how they handled themselves—sometimes even seeing them quarrel. What we remember most vividly is how they always—no matter how strained their feelings might have become—seemed to come back to being *loving* with one another. As kids, we didn't have much of a sense of time. How quickly or how slowly feuding relatives regained their loving attitude, we had no clue about. As kids, we were always active with something or other back then—little league, church choirs, and youth groups—you name it. The time lapses that surely existed went unnoticed. All we knew was that the grownups made amends. And it meant something to them and to the family as a whole to find peace. Was it fun all the time? Of course not. Were there strong arguments? You bet. Was this in any way the always-calm demeanor of Ward & June Cleaver (for those old enough to remember the *Leave It To Beaver* series)? No way. But it all came together—always—at New Year's Eve time.

You've heard of annual rituals—some you have done, or others you have read about—from people and cultures all over the world. The one our family knew best, New Year's Eve, became a major event. Prior to the Times Square countdown on television, the feast included a lot more trimmings (and desserts!) than any normal family get-together. Meal time was early enough to allow for plenty of talk time among the whole family, for more music or impromptu vocal or dance performances by the youngest of us kids, for lots of family friends to drop by, for the football games—the professional one on TV and the marginally permissible one in the living room, and for second and third helpings of whatever we wanted. By most standards, our celebration resembled an indoor picnic in December. No intricate fireworks displays. No fancy decorations. No paid entertainers (we had enough raw talent for a *Star Search* of our own). New Year's Eve revolved around my grandparents' anniversary, but we all understood that it bore much greater significance. When we brought in the new year with a shout, sang *Auld Lang Syne*, and walked around the tables to each person—hugging, kissing, and saying "I love you" to every one—we knew we were a family. No matter what went on throughout the year gone by, this was a time of togetherness and love—and forgiveness.

Whenever times were tough, or when tragedy struck, we witnessed further evidence of our family's unity. A noticeable quality of early family life was that we could openly criticize or mock one another. With so much comic quality in our family DNA, none were exempt from pranks or teasing. Parents and grandparents alike even gave us kids a free pass to respond in kind—that is—to a point. Put-downs flowed, but only as long as they were issued and received in jest. And, so it was, family member to family member. But, heaven help an outsider who tried to do the same!

When my immediate family moved away, a large metropolitan community took the place of our large family network and small community. What an eye-opener! Instead of an eight-room school—kindergarten through sixth grade, one teacher per grade—I enrolled in a school ten times larger. On the first day of school, a loud bell went off at about 8:20 am; almost everyone in my class got up and left, and I had no idea why or where they were going. When I asked where everybody was headed, a kid (who later became a good buddy) told me that this was just "homeroom," that the "first bell" was starting, and that I had five minutes to get to my first class. In that moment, things changed dramatically. School now consisted of a different teacher and room for each class, a huge gym with a locker room, a lunchroom, an auditorium, and kids from a variety of ethnic and racial backgrounds. This was definitely a "Toto, we're not in Kansas anymore" feeling. And my exposure to so much more—both good and bad, but an education in all—was about to unfold.

My brothers and I count ourselves among the fortunate. We had the best of mentors and role models. Our maternal grandfather, Edward Fellows, affectionately known as "Pap," was way ahead of his time. Literally *anyone* who came into his home was welcomed and treated with respect and a loving attitude. The first time I came into close personal contact with a black guy was at Nana and Pap's. "Buzz" was my uncle's good friend. This particular uncle was only nine years my senior, so he and his buddy were about age seventeen. I observed that the color of this man's skin meant nothing to Pap. It was only important that this man felt welcome in Pap's home. He was asked to sit at Pap's end of the table so they could "chat a bit." It left a lasting image in my memory; it later became my mental picture of what brotherhood is all about.

As our patriarch, Pap prayed the family blessing at dinner like no one else did—or has done since—with an earnest voice, tightly closed eyes, showing nothing less than total gratitude to God. His deliberate pauses and inimitable inflections gave clear witness to his tremendous expression of personal belief. Without exception, Pap had a way of making every one of us grandchildren feel special. Even as pre-teens, for example, he would invite us, after dinner, into the back kitchen. It was there that Pap took his customary little bit of sherry (port wine). And, yes, he gave us young men what he called "a little nip" just so we would know we were bona fide members of his special club. We consumed no more than a thimble full, and yet we were at once included in and accepted as the men of the family.

It wasn't until my late teens that I came to understand how this man acquired his natural zest for life and his deep love of family. Pap was the first in our family to leave his home in England for the American dream. He was nineteen, and already had *eight years'* experience working in the coal mines—a skill which he knew he could employ in America. After saving enough money to send for one of his brothers, the two of them quickly earned enough to send for their youngest brother. But, shortly thereafter, Pap heard the call to arms and volunteered to fight in World War I. Most members of my own family are unaware that Pap actually returned to England to enlist. But, he was rejected by the medical examiner there; he needed an appendectomy and a hernia repair which the military doctors refused to perform at that time. So, what did he do? He returned to the United States and explained his condition to the local Army recruiter. He was enlisted on February 13, 1918, had surgery two weeks later, and was transferred to the 37th Machine Gun Division in Cincinnati as soon as he was able to travel. At that same time, the 37th had already received their orders to mobilize. So, his training consisted of "O.J.T.," on-the-job-training on a troop ship bound for France.

Fighting in the third row of infantry as a machine gunner, Pap—along with thousands of others—put his life on the line. In the Argonne Woods of France, he witnessed death, and he emerged with his life and a new understanding of survival. But he also came away from the war knowing that God had been his guardian the entire time. The most vivid examples he shared with me included the artillery shell that did not explode as it landed literally between the legs of the man Pap sat beside while they ate their grass soup (rations were scarce that day). On a very different day, he could only continue shooting from his own position as a mortar shell ripped through the body of his best friend, some five yards away.

Pap also saved the Bible that he carried in his knapsack—the Bible that one day he discovered *had an enemy bullet lodged in it*. If you take a moment or two to reflect on any one of these incidents, you quickly get the sense of this man's faith—faith going into an international crisis, and faith reaffirmed in so many ways during his wartime experience. And, you can appreciate equally well how he may have come to understand what it means to never sweat the small stuff. Pap knew how to live life, and he showed us what it means to be grateful in all circumstances. As kids and as young adults, we never heard him mention what he didn't have—a high school diploma, material wealth, or a car. He always demonstrated his thankfulness for what he had. His passion was his love of God, family, and country. He was a genuine *role model.*

Our Nana was Pap's soft-spoken, humble, and kind-hearted mate. She was naturally pleasant and quiet-spirited. She always wanted to know what she could do to help someone else and always seemed to be cooking a stew or a pot roast—almost always with Yorkshire pudding—and usually for a big crowd. Our Nana had a natural, quiet grace about her. They both had eyes that smiled. These folks weren't financially wealthy, but they had a firm understanding of the riches that they possessed; they were always surrounded by family and close friends.

Only as a parent, especially of teenagers, did I truly begin to see what my parents did for me and what they have come to mean to me. They were always there for their three boys. They kept us busy, or somehow we seemed to be involved in things—school, church, sports, and plenty of extracurricular activities. We had chores starting at an early age. We learned we had to *earn* things. They taught honesty, trust, love, optimism, and Judeo-Christian values. How? By the way they conducted themselves, their manner of speech, and their slowness to lose their cool with us. In other words, they *showed* us. They also gave us the latitude to make our own mistakes—something I know that I exercised a bit more than they had in mind! I made some major blunders. My constant hope any more is to not repeat them and to apologize wherever possible to those I may have hurt along the way. Of all the lessons I gained from this select group of role models, I believe the greatest message was how to love.

For now, I want to begin by offering a symbol and a few words to go along with it. A word picture can be very effective in communicating a message, but a familiar symbol will help to remember it. For example, can you picture Heaven? It seems a senior minister couldn't help but wonder if there were golf courses in Heaven. Through intense prayer on the subject, he got his answer from an angel. Not only were there golf courses, but they were the best—plush greens, groomed fairways, no rain, courteous players, and free caddies. When the minister offered his prayer of thanks for such good news, the angel added, "Yes, great news indeed! And, by the way, we have you down for a tee time this weekend!"

Well, I can't promise you any insight into what Heaven is like, but I would like to give you an earthly picture with a heavenly focus. First, I believe the *wheel* is a helpful tool because it can easily tell us something about how we spend our most precious commodity—time. The wheel suggests that we are constantly on the go. But it also demonstrates for us what happens if we don't maintain a certain sense of *balance* in the things we do or in the things we fail to do. Let me explain.

If you would, think of each spoke on the wheel as representing a key aspect of our lives. What would happen if we chose to live in only one dimension, or if we spent all of our time and energies focusing only on one or two areas? You can be sure this wouldn't be much of a wheel at all. The so-called wheel would be running severely out of round, meaning, if we choose to run our lives this way, we run way out of balance, too.

Let me put some labels on these spokes. Let's say that each spoke represents one of the following areas of our lives: love, family, work, community, and health (in which I include nature). Then let's place God—our personal faith, if you will—in the center.

It may be obvious to you now that for many years I have believed in this simple little word known as *balance*. By maintaining some sense of balance among these pieces of our lives, I am convinced that we can end any given day, or week, or month, with the assurance that we have lived well. Right about now you're going to say, "But what about all those times when we know that the focus simply has to be on just work, or on church-work, or my commitment to a volunteer group?" To your own question, I would add, "What might this mean if you have been living apart from your early religious roots or if you have had no exposure to religion at all?"

I suggest that a simple image such as this can help us get a handle on what we do and why we do it. It can bring us back into balance, especially in those times when we know deep down in our guts that we are running on a particular treadmill with no thought as to why or how to jump off. For example, when guys seem to be doing things away from home a lot, we will hear our spouse or significant other say that we are *never* home. Maybe we play golf once or more per week. If so, we would likely hear the same thing. The question, then, becomes one of how much time we devote to each of the areas on our wheel.

Have you read any good "how-to" articles lately? Have you committed to memory some of the more popular formulas for success or happiness that are out there today? Browse the web using search words such as three ways to healthier living, five secrets to success, seven habits of effective people, or ten keys to a happy life, and see how many pop up! I offer you this image of the wheel and six aspects for a man to focus on. But, I also welcome you to consider your own top five or six focal points as you go along with me here.

Just as I believe it is within us to live each day one at a time and to take each day as a gift, I believe *each week* can and should include some time for each point on the wheel—each area of our lives. Now will you turn with me and look at the hub of the wheel? As a sneak peek into several of these chapters, let me say right up front that I have placed God in the center and for good reason. More accurately, I believe God has always been in the center. It just may take a while for some of us to recognize this fact from personal experience.

Another way to look at these spokes is to see them without the wheel, yielding the image I prefer, a *star*. I see it like this:

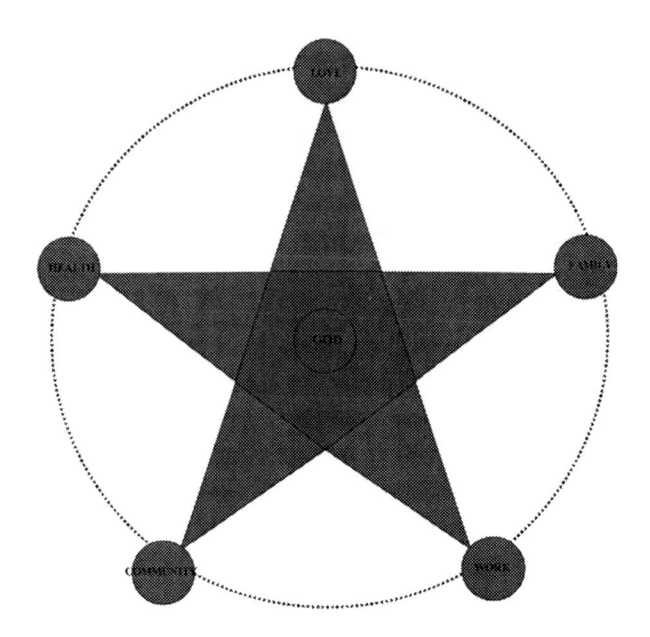

Going back to the same descriptions used for each spoke, can you now visualize these points on the star as key aspects of a happy and meaningful (even purposeful) life? Overall, I think every one of us knows in his heart that each area is very important. But, have we taken the time to define and keep focused on our key elements? Here is a chance to refine your focal points or to develop them.

My wish for you is that you can find enough meaning within these pages to become what I would call a *Star Man*. And just what would that be? Well, for starters, it would be a man who knows his priorities and who stays focused on them. It would include a man who is aware of a Higher Power or who at least has begun to think about God's role in his life. As we proceed through these pages, I believe the additional attributes of a *Star Man* will be revealed. Without a frame of reference and without real-life circumstances that we can all relate to, I'm sure that such a notion would simply fall idle. So, I invite you in to explore some real-world episodes with me. As you do, examine the principles for yourself; consider your own perspectives. Determine what parallels you may have seen and draw from them whatever you can. Even more importantly, I encourage you to formulate your own set of guidelines—your star points—something in your own words and handwriting that you can use as a personal road map. Let me say again that I believe that a man's personal plans must have a strong spiritual center. Then, once you decide what your personal guideposts are, you have something to refer back to as often as you need. Furthermore, if you check in with your personal list on a regular basis, I am confident that you will discover new rewards that you had not thought of. You are also likely to find yourself doing the things that you yourself have said are priorities.

Speaking man-to-man, as we will do throughout this book, I confess that my notion of a *Star Man* is actually a derivative term. As an undergrad student at West Point, I discovered that a Star Man was a guy (no women back then) who ranked in the top five percent of our class academically. Much as I may have liked the sound of the words star man, my grades were nowhere near that level of overall performance—not even close. As with many of my fellow students, I preferred to think of myself as ranking among the *top 80%* of the class!

Going back to our image, let's nail down this idea of a *Star Man* now. The point is, in many respects, you are already doing some of the things which you know to be the *right* things. You have personal attributes and gifts that you employ every day. Let something within these chapters be an encouragement to you. Visualize yourself as a *Star Man*.

If you pay attention to each of these aspects of your daily or weekly life, I believe you will be amazed at how much peace you come to know. Whenever I find myself ignoring any one aspect of the star for an extended period of time, I find myself wondering why I don't feel as *happy or fulfilled*. I am not as energetic, cheerful, or enthusiastic about all that is happening in my life as I know I can be. I'm just a grump.

From our earlier example of being away from home a lot, do you feel you are *missing something* when you haven't had any contact with your wife or your significant other? For you dads, does the same hold true if you have gone several days without contact with your children? We must recognize these pangs as being quite normal. We also need a coping, balancing mechanism. Even though we are not likely to touch on all of these priority areas in our daily lives, I remain confident that we can do a little something for each aspect in the course of every *week*. With the idea of maintaining *balance* firmly in mind, we are ready to take a closer look at each point on our star.

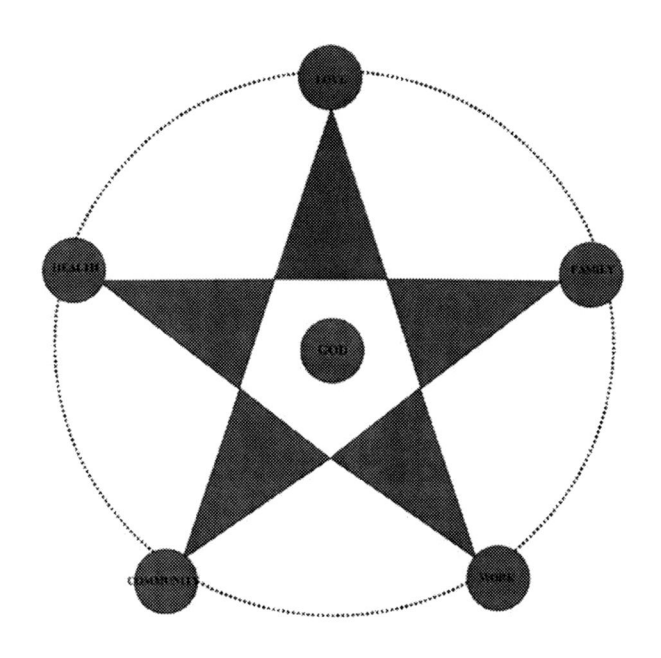

Love

I heard this simple yet insightful phrase from a presentation I attended years ago. It came from Denis Waitley, author and motivational speaker. The phrase he used was what I would call a concise definition of love. He described love as meaning "looking for good." Try saying that to yourself—looking for good. Sounds pretty simple, doesn't it?

If I love you, I see the good in you, and so I let that positive, pre-disposed attitude toward you dominate my thinking. A good friend once described love this way, "Love gives." Even though my loving relationship with someone goes through some trials, arguments, or any other antagonistic behaviors, I am able to come back to the central point of loving the other person. Most assuredly, our commitment to one another will be put to the test. None of us can escape tensions or interpersonal conflicts. How we deal with them makes all the difference in a nurturing, healthy relationship.

Intuitively, we all know these following statements to be true. They are one-liners that help us remember how we should conduct ourselves:

- Love your God, your family, and your neighbor just as you love yourself.
- Love is sacrificing your own wants or needs to attend to the needs of others.
- Better to have loved and lost, than never to have loved at all.
- A life without love is very empty and sad.

In terms of personal conduct, the hardest part about love for me to talk about is love within the context of marriage. The key question comes down to this: How well do we show love for the person who is our life-long mate? Having a couple of decades of adult life under my belt, I still find it a bit difficult now to adequately describe what I experienced in my twenties and thirties. My first marriage resulted in divorce. Thinking of my second marriage—some fifteen years later and going strong—I find it very easy to relate to you what it means to me today.

See if this speaks to you in some way.

In my twenties, I thought my spouse and I were among the people who had arrived at a stage of maturity well beyond our actual years. High school was a distant memory, and we had started earning our own way and experienced college. From a man's point of view, somehow a college diploma and a new career gave a guy quite a boost! A man might also notice a new-found strut in his stride. The reality of the situation was that our education had just begun. So exactly *how mature* were we then?

I don't know about you, but I would imagine that the timing of this differs for all of us. After about ten years of working and having started a family, my spouse and I thought we had it all. We were rocking along in so many ways—socially, spiritually, somewhat financially, and emotionally. As I look back on it now, I can see that what we really tended to do in our relationship was to *trade* good deeds with one another, rather than just *give* to each other. Over time, we also lost trust and mutual respect and quite often some levels of self-respect. Within our individual thoughts, we both knew we wanted children. And however limited our skills as parents may have been, we loved and continue to love our daughters.

Guys don't talk about it much, but we hear women and almost every daytime talk show host gab about it—the love of a soul-mate. Sounds like a cliché, right? At this point in our lives, I can say without hesitation that my wife and I are soul-mates. Before I even try to articulate what this means, keep in mind that guys only do the Cliffs Notes version of this kind of stuff. My description of having a true soul-mate goes something like this: caring, giving or sacrificing, supporting, touching, holding, and valuing. You might observe that all of these words require some sort of action on our part. Right! Furthermore, they all hinge on love and respect.

Caring suggests giving enough effort to make sure all the physical support needs are provided, but it extends much further. Caring always means demonstrating concern for each others' needs, wants, or general well-being. Caring allows room to ask each other questions or to offer each other observations or suggestions.

Caring also consists of doing some of the little things, without being asked. The things I am referring to may be as small as emptying the dishwasher or taking out the trash without being asked to do it. Perhaps you have been known to fill your mate's car with gas or have it serviced without even mentioning it. Doing some of her desired "little projects"—somehow knowing that they are not little to her—would be another way of showing how much you care. Suppose you stayed home so you could have some together time instead of sticking to your schedule or routine? What positive affirmation of your relationship!

Question: Have you figured out that men are very different from women? If you have any doubt at all, let me suggest you sit down with a copy of John Gray's book, *Men Are From Mars, Women Are From Venus: A Practical Guide for Improving Communication and Getting What You Want in Your Relationships*. Allow me to confirm one of Gray's claims. If you are going to respond to your wife or your significant other, even if she is your soul-mate, you would be wise to avoid the trap of offering advice. Yes, she asked you for it, but be careful. You heard her words, but you missed her *meaning*. So, what is a man to do? Give her a hug, a nod of acknowledgement, an attentive ear; but avoid offering advice, unless you are absolutely sure that is what she is really after.

For me, it is amazing how easy doing the little things can be. I genuinely want to pay attention to this matter, and my wife does too. In my personal case, these simple acts of thoughtfulness stem from understanding a key element in my spouse's personal make up: her deep appreciation for doing the little things. And, it cuts both ways. I am at my best, and feel I am doing my best, when I know she feels loved and appreciated. It's a wonderful, cyclical pattern which fuels itself.

Both giving and sacrificing, I think, are intertwined. In guy terms, day-to-day, these verbs suggest putting off something from our own personal to-do list, and instead, doing what our partner feels is needed. In plain English, sacrificing entails putting her first. As you do so, don't be surprised that somehow, magically, your projects still end up getting done, and exactly when they are completed becomes irrelevant. If this is already part of your make-up as a couple, you know exactly what I am talking about here. Guys, whether or not you are married, engaged, or devoted to one woman, this little tidbit comes in handy in *any* relationship. If this is not a regular practice with you, try it a few times and see what happens. I am convinced that you will witness her making these same types of little sacrifices, which again only serve to reinforce and reaffirm your needs or wants as being equally important. And so the cycle of loving and caring continues and grows.

Just in case you think this sounds a bit surreal, let me assure you that it is not. My spouse and I have our different agendas and our tugs of war; our seemingly urgent needs can and do clash. Have you experienced this phenomenon in your household? I recall a particular vacation which I felt was best spent seeing as much as we could of our nation's capital—the National Archives, the National Art Gallery, the Mall, and a performance at Kennedy Center. My wife had other ideas. It seems she had the notion to go gem mining in North Carolina. (Oh, joy! Why not go to one of those "alligator farms" in rural Georgia?) So, what did we do? You guessed it. After three days in Washington, we were panning for not-so-precious stones in a creek bed no wider than my bath tub. But, hey, don't be so quick to laugh. Do you recall a time or two when you were absolutely right about your own sense of priorities? And what did you do? I'll wager that you dug your heels in and insisted on having your own way; then, after some minutes had passed, you got smart too. Call it compromise.

On rare occasions, we discovered, common ground just could not be found. So, we typically continued on our individual agendas and let it go. Fortunately, there has never been an episode when we attempted to force one another to change directions. I assure you that it didn't take long for both of us to realize and acknowledge that the issue wasn't such a big deal as we made it at the time.

So, what does it mean to be supportive of one another? Though support may take on many forms, I believe emotional and spiritual support are the most important—if not critical. When I have a series of trials or tough times, even *during* them I have a sense I will find solace when I get home. My consolation might come from the comfort of conversation about the events of the day. Or, maybe just a listening ear or a period of solitude will settle me down from the turmoil. To be supported like that gives me such a sense of confidence, strength, and endurance that is truly hard to describe. The beauty is that support works in both directions, and we both know it.

Part of our male genetic make-up is an awareness of financially supporting our spouse and family. But do we also consider the support we give our spouses in social situations? One easy example: No matter how long we have been married, I am going to hold the door, offer a hand, walk on the traffic side of the sidewalk, and basically make sure my wife knows she is the lady of the house. Guys, to do less, I believe, would deny her the proper courtesy and respect. Trite and old fashioned, you say? Today's women don't need or want that kind of thing. Think again.

When it comes to work-related issues that are bothering us, soul-mates can be wonderful sources of stress relief. But, how often do we talk about them? I believe this phenomenon works in both directions. She is your sounding board; you are hers. Just hearing yourself express specific concerns you will usually hear the real issue or discover another solution.

Say, for example, the lady of your house is on a roller-coaster ride with a local automobile repair shop. She has become noticeably upset and frustrated—your opportunity to lend support. Your offer to visit the shop together with her to deal with the problem may or may not be accepted. Your gesture alone may be all it takes to reinforce your spouse. How many similar examples or situations did you just think of?

As in the description of caring, some of the little forms of support are really big—doing an errand that she doesn't have time for, taking time off workdays to go to the doctor's office together, quietly picking up a household bill that she is expecting, and paying it without talking about it. The watchdog question here is this: How do I support or build up my soul-mate so that she can be her *best self?*

The notion of giving true support often reveals itself in social situations. How often have you heard supposedly loving couples put each other down in public? How often have you felt this kind of sting from someone who claims to love you? Whether such actions are done with the other person present or not, they only serve to tear away a piece of the relationship. They surely destroy an intimate relationship. Candidly, guys, I've done this wrong and I've done it right. Maybe you have, too. Being able to control our tongues is the way to do it right; and, we know that sometimes biting our tongues is the hardest thing to do. When we truly care about each others' feelings and self-worth, maybe it isn't so hard to do after all.

Touching and holding our mate are not just as things men should think of from time to time. Both are a means of very effective communication. For instance, if she moves away from you quickly, you can bet she has a reason! Even a quick, unsolicited hug or a simple touch can tell you volumes about how she is doing. This one small gesture will also tell you how *you* are doing and whether or not any troubles are brewing—whether or not you caused them or even knew about them! Before I say something more about cause and effect, let me add another personal note.

Figuratively, you touch others all the time. Remember that a simple phone call, card, note, or visit, especially when you know people need it—sometimes desperately—is a wonderful way of touching them. You touch their hearts. I would also say this. Just do it, and then go on about your business. Remember, too, that it serves no good purpose to talk to others about what you have done. Just be glad about it in your own heart. Isn't that what the idea of random acts of kindness is all about? I am extremely pleased to say that I have now witnessed my daughters doing these very things. It is personally gratifying now to know that they actually do so more often than I will ever know.

Do you know you can also touch someone with just a look? I believe we touch others and communicate loudly with them through our eyes. The old romanticist who penned the notion of the eyes being windows to the heart and soul was absolutely right. You can read joy, pain, depression, loneliness, and excitement in others' eyes, and you show these emotions in your own. You learn to read each other the more time you spend together. I am convinced that something as simple as a warm glance can turn someone's day around completely.

So, how do you learn to read your soul-mate? Ah, now such ability is a gift which comes only from spending focused time together. Sorry, guys, no short-cuts available.

As for the physical touching part, I guess my wife won't mind too much if I go out on a limb here. Being what I call premature empty nesters, we have had several years to improve on the ways we stay connected to each other. For instance, our morning hug, typically in the kitchen, waiting for the coffee to finish perking, has become something of a ritual in our house. On the surface, this would seem to be a silly little routine; but it's not. Starting the day off with a warm hug like that gives us a real boost—an affirmation of our bond.

Guys need to clown around some, too. I have a lot of fun waiting for my wife to get up on a step stool or into some equally vulnerable position, so I can move in for an unexpected pinch. Whatever your preferred antics might be, you can be sure that they convey a healthy and loving message. Such small doses of reassurance go a long way. You say you're really not into doing anything like that and don't really know where to start? Use your imagination.

Valuing each other—and showing it—has everything to do with *respect*. If it's true, as Denis Waitley asserted years ago, that love really means "look for the good," then it must also hold true that we men are called to share in, if not lead, the actions that comprise loving behavior—giving of ourselves freely and with joy, genuinely caring, actively listening, and regarding each other's beliefs, feelings, or concerns as being *most important*—all in order to affirm that we truly value each other.

Frankly, in any wholesome relationship, if you can't say yes to these aspects of loving behavior, then it may be time to really check yourself out and consider how you really value your mate. More than that, ask yourself these two questions: Does your partner know how you feel about her? If so, *how* does she know?

Guys, we always get to choose how we show love for our mate. At the moment you know deep down that something needs to be said or done, it's too easy to just let it go and not think too much about it. I believe you get hurt—longer, harder, deeper—by not examining these things for yourself.

Some noteworthy scholars and behavioral scientists say that having love in our lives is pivotal—even crucial—for us to feel happy and fully alive. I wholeheartedly agree. I would also say that the love of others, and especially a soul-mate, helps men approach all other areas of our lives with incredible confidence. The area most closely linked to love with a soul-mate is love within the family.

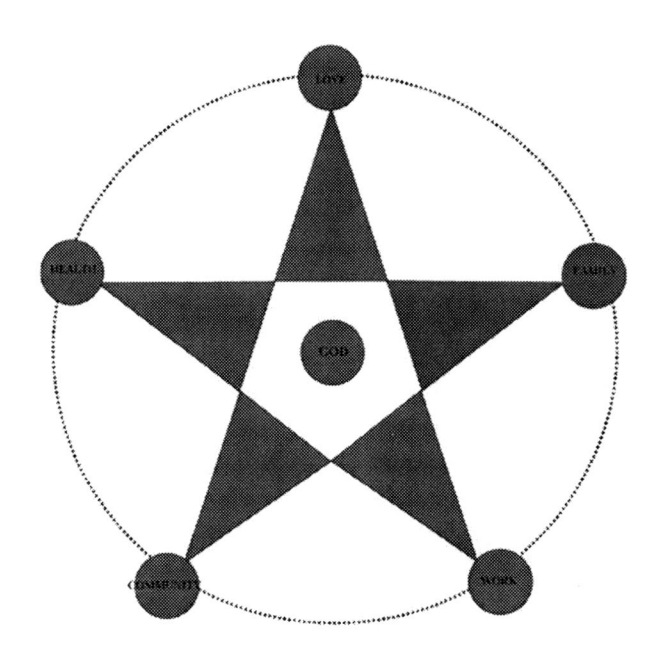

Family

Every once in a while we encounter guys who wonder why they just weren't *born* right. Well, obviously that's not a very sensible thing to dwell on. We don't get to choose our parents, grandparents, or other relatives. Nor are we able to choose many of our experiences. At its very best, your family is the place you can just be yourself. You are in a place where you are one hundred percent sure to find love, nurture, and the support that you need *no matter what*. At its best, your family provides a place where all of these things abound, plus a few others—fun, laughter, playfulness, and time together. Consider also when families are at their worst. You find that love, rules, morals, principles, God, security, safety, health, and a whole lot of other life support needs are absent or nonexistent.

I'm guessing that your family was and is something in between. Here is a big surprise for you—so is just about everyone else's! As a young parent, I never thought too much about this. I had always just assumed that the family I reared would be a lot like the one I grew up in, obviously with some improvements of my own. With children now grown and living independently, I find it a bit challenging to retrace the good and bad features of our family environment that I have been responsible for. But several things do stand out.

As a young dad, I loved that we were an outdoors, get-out-and-go-discover-things family. Did we spend time with indoor games? Of course we did. Two particular bedrooms I can think of were littered with a collection of china dolls, an assortment of My Little Pony characters, or a miniature house full of Winnie the Pooh figures. So, my daughters definitely had indoor interests. But I'm so thankful that Game-Boys, Nintendo, and equivalent mind-numbing games were not as popular then as they are now. I believe these can be real family-killers today, not to mention the impact on kids who sit idle in front of a computer monitor for hours. I am equally concerned about children and youth who are over-exposed to television. Where cable channels are ubiquitous and increasingly distasteful, I see even greater danger in unsupervised viewing. But, my point here is this: Pick up the thing we call a remote. Sit back and observe how it is being used, and I think you'll find that it is really just a device that keeps the members of our families, both young and old, *remote* from one another.

From our family's standpoint, divorce brought on more minuses than I can adequately describe. In wanting to offer straight guy-talk, I do not want to spend too much time on the personal hurts, the lessons, and the inner growth that come from the breakdown of a marriage and a family unit. My ex-spouse and I both contributed to the eventual break-up. Whether drinking or partying too much was a factor, I can't really say. No doubt that these didn't help matters any. Overall, we failed to show each other the mutual love and respect that we both deserved. In terms of impact on my family, one of the most significant difficulties—which was also the most lasting source of hurt and frustration—was the new reality of how precious little time my daughters and I would have together. Without turning this into a treatise on the legal system, I would like to put my concern about time into proper perspective.

In the mid-nineteen eighties, our social-judicial system seemed predisposed to favor the mother when deciding custody issues or financial support matters. In many regions of the country, the situation does not appear to be much different today. Regardless of the local application of such laws in your area, I am certain that a guy's best approach to the courts is through the qualified, relevant experience of an attorney.

Now, before some of you go jumping on this bandwagon, this is not my way of spewing out sour grapes commentary. It is simply a portrayal of the laws and local practices of that period in a specific domestic court. Let me also say to you very candidly that my own naiveté and short-sightedness as to how divorce arrangements *really* worked played a huge role in the way our family time played out. The short version of the agreement that I signed included: every other weekend with the children, alternating major holidays, and two weeks each summer. What I did not anticipate were the unwritten or unspecified rules—for example, no provisions, and therefore no assurances, made for the children's time with their grandparents and with my relatives in general, no accountability requirements as to how child support funds were used, and ultimately no real say in major decisions such as choice of schools, classes, or their continued religious training.

As I said, time was the main issue. The time that we did have together, especially in their formative years, was extremely short. Just as the old cliché implies, it just flew by. But something else happened, too. Behaviors changed. Over time, my children came to understand that Dad's house rules were really just temporary, since, after all, they would only be with me for the weekend. I could invoke a rule here or a punishment there, but within a day or two they would be back with their mother. Any continuance there of my disciplinary action would have been purely coincidental back then. So, how was Dad to render a judgment and make it stick? As the Dad in this case, I can assure you that discipline was not what I ever wanted to focus on—not when our time together was already so short. I never planned a weekend with that in mind. But, I felt then—and feel now—that their understanding of proper conduct, manners, and behavior, were too important to let slide. So, we worked through all of the confrontations you can imagine.

When my children were growing, in the three through eight year old range, I wanted to *do it all*, and even then thought I was actually balancing my priorities. In the truest sense of a dad's duty to his family, I thought I was living the traditional man's role. A major adjustment that I'm sure I never made properly was in the amount of time consumed by work-related travel. Still pretty new out of the military, I was a rather stubborn perfectionist. Willingness to travel on business emerged as the ladder to career growth, and I embraced it. And technical sales also meant more income. Unfortunately for our family, I lost my focus, and probably did so while convincing myself that I had it all in proper perspective. I ran out of balance.

I still see myself, for example, mowing the backyard of our house in the southern suburb of Pittsburgh with a daughter in my lap helping me steer, but only for a little while. You see, I had this half-acre of grass to mow, before eating quickly, showering, watching some TV (there's that *remote* thing again), going to bed, and getting up early for an overnight business trip. What made me think that there just wasn't enough time to stop the mower, get off, and play with the girls on the really cool wooden play gym and swing set we had? Or, why not join them in our six foot by six foot sandbox? I did what I felt had to be done at the time. Even on weekends I routinely felt the conflicted notions of necessary home improvement projects versus fun family time. My mixed priorities became fairly easy to spot these many years later.

While we were all together as a young family, one thing we did was attend church together. As some older teenagers do, my girls chose not to continue participating in church life. Deep down, I know they have a foundation of belief in God and a sense of the importance of regular worship. I just keep praying that the Spirit will lead them back to a personal connection with God—the sooner the better. Whenever we're together, you can be sure I issue some form of question or reminder about this. I hope to be *showing* them something of God's love as well.

Something else about their childhood upbringing has proven very important. My daughters were born into a big family. We had get-togethers at least every other week. While we could never seem to duplicate the ones I grew up with at my grandparent's house, these occasions were no less meaningful to my own children. Whenever the kids mixed with adult relatives, especially aunts and uncles, something really special happened. They watched each other constantly. They often listened to each other more—at least differently. There were periods when the kids and the non-parent grownups were more open or more candid with each other. And family stories seemed limitless. Personal episodes that kids got to hear—stories about these adults who were now their elders—played a role in shaping each young person. More than that, stories molded our family. They drew us closer—for life—and they demonstrated what a bond feels like. We didn't grasp the full significance then. But we get it now.

Grandparents are even cooler with respect to children. Who knows better than a grandparent how to make a fuss over children and make them feel special and loved? Among a dad's biggest wishes for his own children is that they have an opportunity to benefit from *whole-family* exposure and time together. I certainly hope that my daughters see to it for their own children. Even beyond the love and nurturing—beyond the structural support and roots that young children receive—the immediate family and the greater family enable our children to grow up with a deep feeling of security and confidence that nothing else can replace or duplicate.

Now is a good time to pause for a question. Do you have a personal sense of the importance of this family structure, either from direct personal experience or from a later understanding of how this may have been lacking somewhere in your past? Possibly *you* are the kind of guy who has reservations about assimilating into a larger family. If so, you might wonder how to blend in while maintaining your own unique identity. Maybe some of your older family members have already been there at one time and would have some wise words to offer you on the subject. Being extraverted would be a plus in this situation. If you are introverted, you might have to seek out other family introverts as a starting point. In any case, it's yours to recognize, and it is yours to commence working on.

Anytime I'm back together with my brothers, cousins, aunts, or uncles, it takes all of about five minutes to become fully aware of the good memories among us. Then the longer we are all together and the more we talk, the more memories and stories come streaming out. If you are lucky, you have witnessed this yourself. During such family times, what we really rekindle is a state of mind. We reaffirm a certain bond that can never be broken. Trust and love are always present. We are *home*.

Children of broken families often know best how having divorced parents has affected their concept of family. All of a sudden, and without any experience to know how to react, they may even become part of a new family—a blended family if you will. When my ex-spouse remarried, my time with the kids grew even more splintered. The girls were literally carried off in several new directions.

Unfortunately for them, their time also became a matter of control by the custodial parent. It suddenly became too inconvenient, for example, to keep shifting the girls back and forth—packing and unpacking each time—ensuring they had all the belongings they needed in both houses. While the children may have seemed remarkably resilient, I believe these times were most often very strained by any number of emotional issues brewing under the surface. I do not wish to speculate what the social scientists are saying about this today. What I know unquestionably is that divorce has a definite impact on young children. While the effect may not be devastating, it is a factor to be considered as they are thrown into a potential whirlwind of new family relationships.

For a moment, let's stop and consider that new or blended family relationships may be very difficult for some children to adjust to. With very limited perspective in this area, I can only surmise that this is where a guy needs to be fully engaged in the process and needs to consider inputs from counselors or other professionals wherever possible.

I don't know about you, but overall I wouldn't say that I have had what you would call a tough life. Yes, my background included a near-crippling or near-death experience as an older teenager, a disabling injury during college years, and later the pain and the emotional roller coaster ride of divorce. I know now that my *number one challenge* was to keep on being the Dad to my own children. When I did not live in the same house with them 24/7/365, and when I became the so-called joint custodial parent, this grew infinitely harder to do as my daughters matured. By living within—and persevering through—this legal description of joint parenting, I found no real support in enforcing my rights as the joint custodial parent. The whole aspect of being a part-time Dad was something I never dreamed of or expected in my life. Trust me, it was never a goal. Today I view that period as having been a deep, emotional tug of war. Throughout several years, post-divorce, I continually focused on making the best out of this new living arrangement. Judging from the way my ex-spouse and I interacted, we both experienced new revelations in the aftermath of our decision. New realities set in.

Despite all the turbulence, I still wanted to share with my daughters some other key events in my own life. Scores of travel stories and often some of my own feelings and beliefs just never seemed to be told. Time had a way of working against us.

Let me go no further without saying a word here to *all* guys. A lot of you may have never experienced this issue of family time and communications. But, widely published statistics tell us that about fifty percent of the marriages in this country end in divorce; so, many of you can relate to this personally. But, let's leave the topic of divorce. Let's not forget about some of us dads who can also become *emotionally divorced* from the family. Are you working so many hours a day that little or no time is left for our kids? Do you take on so much overnight travel that your quality time is relegated to phone calls, emails, or text messages?

This point about time bears repeating. My daughters and I spent a lot of time together, mostly with me listening to what they had on their minds. So often, I wanted to let my daughters know what was going on in my life, too—always the good news but sometimes even the things that can be hard to hear or understand. For example, I vividly recall wanting to go back over the time when they were first told of their parents' intentions to divorce. We never discussed the episode until years later. Even the event itself was about time. I returned home from a four day trip to New Jersey (time away). Upon my return home from that particular week's work, my ex-spouse and I had agreed to have a family meeting. That night, we were going to sit the girls down and explain what was about to happen as best we could. The *"we"* never happened. Prior to my arrival, the girls received the initial news from their mother alone (time missed). To make matters worse, I made only a feeble attempt at trying to talk in private with the girls (time not taken). We don't get do-overs. But if I got one, I'd surely have taken the time to have that talk—all of us together, just like we planned—so there would be no doubt as to what was communicated and how.

We dads can beat ourselves up pretty good about talking or—more likely—not talking, can't we? If my kids' memory of those years shows that I often seemed tense, nervous, or irritated, it could only have been for one reason—I was! Our time was always so very short. I wanted it to be perfect and fun-filled. It never could be all that I had hoped, but I envisioned each of our weekends together with perpetual optimism. Whenever I dropped them off on Sunday evenings, at 6 p.m. sharp, do you think I would let them see my tears? Heck, no! I wouldn't show them that, especially not as a parting impression. And when the Sunday evening drive home was back to Virginia, they also wouldn't know how much my heart ached. I was torn between all the things we didn't do or I didn't say; yet, all the while, I also knew I had reason to be thankful for the time we did have.

A full ten years later—thank God—my relationship with the girls was fully restored. I love the fact that we have evolved into more forward-focused discussions and debates. They constantly remind me that I am still too old-fashioned. But I cherish every discussion we have. This was quite literally ten years of prayers—prayers answered.

These personal glimpses have provided only a few insights into the importance of family, the second point on our star. Before we move on to the next area, I wonder if you have taken the time to reflect on your own family life. Speaking man to man, I can't help but wonder if you have taken the opportunity to be open with people you know well concerning your family stories and experiences.

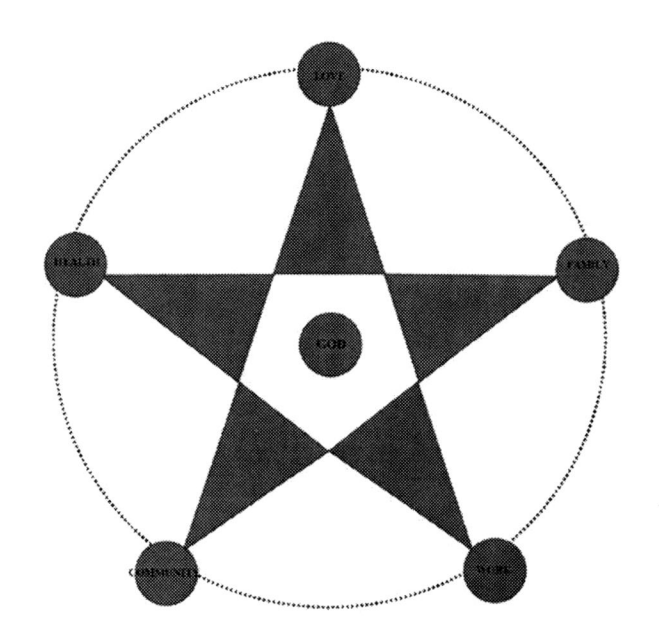

Work

Several years ago I read a little expression that sent my mind racing in circles of reflective thoughts faster than a NASCAR lap. The saying comes from John Piper's book titled: *Desiring God, Meditations of a Christian Hedonist*. Piper drives his point home by asking a few questions—questions that I believe every man should ask himself. How do you answer them? Be honest!

Do I steal [or cheat] to *get*?

Or

Do I work to *get*?

Or

Do I work to get, in order to *give*?

What Piper addresses is our need to assess our *motivation* for the work we do—work for which we are paid. My editorial comment here: We all enter work life full of some form of ambition. Men may even have great aspirations for fame, lofty titles, or money. This catchy phrase is intended to make us think not just about what we are doing, but also why we are doing it.

Allow me to reinforce Piper's point using questions that may hit closer to home: How do I use the money I earn? Is it to buy more "stuff" or toys? Do I take lots of fun trips, maybe even to far-away places? Does my income enable me to play all the best golf courses in the world? Am I driven to live in the best house or neighborhood? And, do I use the money to keep my home looking fresh by continuously remodeling it? If I don't spend much, but save a lot, am I doing so to become independently wealthy?

Among the most misguided messages I've ever seen was on a bumper sticker. It read: He who dies with the most toys wins. Wins what, exactly? As I earn as much as I can, is it so I can have all the things that everybody else seems to have or want? If we had to identify the most popular messages from contemporary media, the list would include: the latest and greatest car, the highest quality sound system, a plasma HDTV—naturally including a universal remote for all my other gadgets, a designer wardrobe, the fastest computer system, or a sophisticated personal jewelry collection. This list could have no end.

"Or do I work to get, in order to give?" Now this is a great and telling question, isn't it? From a man's perspective, what exactly does this mean? Can this be one indicator of a *Star Man*? I think so. For starters, men want to be thought of and recognized as being good providers. The trouble comes when we find so many different views as to what that entails. And, by the way, most of the ideas about giving *things*—which you see on television or read about in the local newspapers, magazines, and other brag rags—are dead end roads.

For example, as I have mentioned earlier, I was an officer in the military. Maybe because of the inherent prestige of a West Point education and training, I felt accepted by others outside of the military circles. Even in the post-Viet Nam era, the academy was a plus on any resume. However, I also encountered several potential employers who readily associated junior military officers with production supervisors or team leaders in the civilian working world. So, we were not necessarily seen as world-class income earners, but in any social order we held our own. At that time of my life and at my level of social awareness, I only knew that my West Point opportunity was the best thing that happened for me. I was lucky to have made it in—even luckier to have graduated. Among my co-workers in those early career years, I was secure and confident. Money had its place, but it wasn't *first place*.

Then I wanted to do *more* for my young family. I got the notion that I wanted to quit relocating so much, as well. Ironically, moving up the corporate ladder meant moving a lot, too. In twenty years, I made a total of sixteen moves!

I have always seen the work I do as a means to an end. And, yes, early on I bought right into the idea of working, so we (really *I*) could start acquiring *things*. By the grace of God, after five years of active duty in the military, I found myself in technical sales, product management, and then marketing, all of which I have greatly enjoyed. But the total truth is, work life is not without its share of sacrifices. Mine was business travel, which meant time away from home and my family. I distinctly remember that my Dad traveled quite a bit, too, especially when my brothers and I were teenagers. He would often be out Monday through Friday on jobs as a bank examiner; Comptroller of the Currency was the official title, working for the Federal Government, Department of the Treasury. To me, being willing to travel on business was simply a natural form of bread-winning that the husband and dad did. I learned that business travel could be especially rewarding, and the subliminal message was that the more travel I was willing to take on the better the financial rewards became. No doubt that work life can have an effect on us when travel is involved. But if your work life does not involve overnight travel, don't get too comfortable just yet. Are you equally absent from family involvement if you are working twelve-hour days? What is left for the family if you work a more reasonable ten hours, then face a ninety-minute commute each way?

Let's be brutally honest. Wherever we guys choose to apply ourselves, the amount of time we devote to it really is up to us. You can refute that statement if you like; I might agree with a few of you. In rare instances, practical alternatives simply do not exist. But in the majority of cases, guys come up with a hundred or so good reasons why they are simply stuck where they work—trapped if you will.

To them, and possibly to you now, I ask: Are you truly in a quandary, or have you given up trying to find a better avenue? Basically, have you given up?

While our work life is one of the key points on our star, time utilization and financial motivation are but two of the areas we could address here. For guys who earn a living, our work lives account for the majority of our waking hours. Together, we could fill volumes with other key issues which create tension or priority challenges. What I want to be sure to share are some insights as to the way we men conduct ourselves at work. Is it different from the way we conduct ourselves anywhere else? What kind of message do we give to others by what we say and what we do?

At the very basic level, we all have got to be dependable. Starting times are to be respected. We are to give a full day's work for a full day's pay. These are fundamentals—minimum standards. Our attitude toward them speaks volumes about us. Want another perspective? These same basic principles apply even if you are self-employed. I encourage every man to think of his work life as self-employment. You see, it is always up to us to work smart enough and hard enough to create our own success. This is another one of those universal laws. The more diligent we are, the luckier we get when it comes to advancement, business growth, incentive awards, bonuses, special perks, and fringe benefits. Luck has nothing to do with it.

Having said all that, I will also offer a news flash: *It will not always work out that way.*

At least for some period of time, you will witness people who give less of themselves. Co-workers who might even be known as slackers move ahead of you or at least advance at the same rate you do. Some will not concern themselves with the job at hand, but they will apply their gift of politicking. Perhaps you will recognize attributes such as these in their more basic descriptive forms—dead wood, brown-nose, and fair-haired boy, come to mind. These employees will advance. You may even observe cases of social promotion, where ethnic origin, race, or sex may become the ultimate tie-breaker that causes you to lose a promotion. Well, should any of these situations occur in your work place, welcome to real-life experience. Things are not always fair. Nor were you ever promised they would be. Now, before you allow this fact to let you become cynical, hear the good news.

We all, at various times in our lives and in our careers, get our time in the sun! Let me say this again. We all have our days in the limelight. This, I believe, is another universal law—the law of averages—which is fairly comforting. It suggests that we will be recognized at various times and for various good reasons throughout our working careers. The hard part for each of us and yet the simple trick is to truly understand this and believe in it. It also requires a tremendous amount of patience. I think that is the toughest part of all—waiting. For most of my work years, I promise you that my competitive instincts kicked in, and I was off and running to win whatever it was that I believed was worth striving for. So how does the competitive-minded guy react to adverse situations such as these? He may well consider other employment. But he also may do the hard work of self-examination and adaptation in order to progress where he is.

It sure would be great to be able to end my commentary right there. But that would be deceitful. I promised you plain talk. My personal walk through what we call our work life has definitely not gone the way of patience, understanding, compromise, or even willingness to change. It seems I've always had two character flaws (at least) at work. As I said, I have seldom been patient. Second, I tend to look hard at the people I work with and even more closely at those I work for. If I ever arrive at a conclusion that they are not as honest, fair-minded, progressive-thinking, decent, or otherwise respectable, as I think they should be, then I find a way to separate myself from them in terms of organizational structure, or I move away from them physically or geographically. Now, this introduces a real key piece of self-incrimination. In two very vivid instances, I was criticized by the person I worked for as sometimes appearing arrogant, aloof, or just plain too cocky for his liking. In truth, it was because I never cow towed to their beliefs or ideas just to keep my job. Although I preferred to be thought of in a good light, I did not spend a whole lot of time pondering how they believed certain situations or issues should have been dealt with. To help clarify, let me say that these differences were always in some way related to people. In the business world, as in most other arenas, it all boiled down to how we treat other people. Whether we were dealing with customers, suppliers, co-workers, executives or owners, I found no room for intimidation, abusive language, disrespect, or manipulation. It's no surprise that I got along great with those who shared the same outlook on business conduct. Our values seemed to agree. But some folks took a different approach. We have to exercise what we believe. *You gotta call 'em as you see 'em.*

Sometimes being so forthright will result in guys having to move on to a new position. If so, I encourage you to make such moves deliberately. It pays to think these things through. A little planning and foresight can help a guy make a better job choice the next time around. Then make your move when you are ready.

In your work life, just as in your personal life, I am convinced that it is imperative that you stay true to your core values and beliefs. Your unique set of core principles may not be obvious to you, but work life brings you plenty of opportunities for holding fast to certain basic beliefs and never letting go of them—no matter what happens and no matter how some business owners and managers make their decisions. And, be forewarned, through such episodes you risk being convicted by others as having this wonderful thing called *character*!

Now here comes the "but." But, remember, we also have to take time out every now and then to do a little self-examination. Just as it is important to know yourself, it is also healthy to challenge your own assumptions, beliefs, and prejudices once in a while. The beautiful thing about it is that doing so has no downside. At worst, you will reaffirm who you are with even greater understanding and conviction. At best, you may uncover a newer or deeper meaning to what you knew before.

So, okay, you've got a set of scruples. If it hasn't done so already, I promise your work life will put them to the test. It is one thing to be honest, trustworthy, and productive when the boss is around. It is a test of your character to be equally so when he or she is away. At various times, it may seem harder to maintain our sense of personal values and integrity at work than it is to do the work itself. For example, in an infinite number of ways we are tempted to act or speak out inappropriately. So, I suggest again, know yourself. Know where you stand. Strive to control your tongue.

In addition to the integrity factor, I promise that wherever you work one or two people will seem to rub you the wrong way. The key is how you choose to deal with that person. I have reflected on this notion a great deal, and it is a critical component of our work-related or business-related relationships.

In spite of our best efforts, sometimes business relationships break down. In the early 1990's, I accepted a position as President, US Operations, of a British-based company. This was the number one company that I had been building my manufacturers' rep business around during the previous four or so years. My little company of two people had a territory that stood at about ten percent of their total U.S. income. We grew in those years to account for twenty five-plus percent of their U.S. sales. So, I suppose that was why the owners offered me the job. After consulting with my partner, he agreed to buy me out and continue operating the rep business, which we both felt at the time was a win-win.

I was hired by an older gentleman, truly a Winston Churchill type, who was Managing Director of the company—a prestigious position by their standards, second only to the owners. He had obviously been a close associate of the owners for over twenty years. Things went very well for the U.S. group while my sister group in Canada was not growing. Two things changed shortly after my first full year. My boss replaced the president in Canada, my counterpart there, with a much younger person (I'll call him George) who was an acquaintance of the owners. Soon afterward, my boss retired.

In rapid succession then, my boss' replacement, another friend of the owners, (I'll call him Robert) made some changes of his own. He immediately repositioned George as President for all of North America. These things having been done, Robert then decided that I should now report back to the U.K. through George.

Let me back up a minute and explain that the Canada office took care of all the financial work for both the U.S. and Canada, and they operated the company-owned warehouse and assembly facility there. Our U.S. business consisted only of sales, marketing, and applications-engineering personnel. Within one month, it became apparent that a lot more change was coming, and it was up to George to carry out the new plans. Several new decisions were enough to turn a reasonable man's stomach. He withheld commission payments to the independent rep sales force in the U.S.—my guys—all of whom were compensated solely by commissions. This was in contrast to the Canadian sales force, which consisted mostly of direct payroll employees. They didn't miss a paycheck. Even if you have no accounting experience, you can understand how this decision made the company profits look better month-by-month and how it helped the company with cash flow. The decision also trashed our U.S. office relationship with our reps. Neither George nor Robert chose to act on my verbal and written protests. The owners didn't respond either, despite my formal objections and calls for immediate correction.

Next, George made the unilateral decision to cut the commission rate on larger sales projects for the reps. For example, when one of them was to receive $2,500, the pay was cut to $1,250. By now, you won't be surprised when I say that I was livid when the paychecks stopped coming out on time and when these tactics were employed. After two episodes of reduced commissions—despite the fact that the commission rate was fixed and agreed to when the orders were received—I went ballistic. So, along came Robert. He flew to our U.S. offices so we could discuss the matter.

Legally, they could do these things and get away with it claiming cash-flow difficulties or some other innocent-sounding excuse. Morally and ethically, they were dead meat. After my final call to the owners, insisting that they get involved, no action was taken. I decided then and there what my reaction would be the following morning. I met Robert and George for breakfast, never sat down, tendered my immediate resignation, went into the office, and met personally with my team to let them know what was about to happen. And I never looked back.

To this day, I believe I would have done the exact same thing if I hadn't had a formal employment contract in place prior to accepting the position as president. But, thank God, I did. Within a few days I signed the appropriate documents all in accordance with professional expectations. But I had a strange feeling that this little saga wasn't over. A week later, I learned how keen my instinct had been. By contract, I had a twelve-month severance. However, George informed me that I could accept a six-month severance, or I could try to work through the courts to get the full twelve months (and pay all the legal costs, and possibly wait twelve to eighteen months to see any money). Are you surprised?

Well, the story got even better. The following month I received the billing statement from the company's Corporate American Express card. The card was provided by the company. It was used for direct-bill charges from my bona fide business travels on the company's behalf, all prior to my resignation. It turns out that George had instructed Adam, the Chief Finance Officer, in Canada, not to pay these bona fide expenses. Since the card also bore my name, they simply directed American Express back to me for payment. As best I can tell, this was the final form of sleaze that I witnessed. Unfortunately for the U.S. reps, my former friends and associates, things continued to deteriorate.

I have often wondered why Adam, whom I knew to be an otherwise honorable person, would not have paid the American Express bill anyway. He also did not respond to my calls. As I see it, that became his own behavioral baggage to deal with.

For my part, I tried to maintain contact with the U.S. reps through these issues. The largest rep, my ex-partner, was among the hardest hit by these unethical practices. He was among the U.S. reps who felt as though I let them down—by not fighting more, or harder, or longer, or something. The sad reality was that nothing would happen without the owners' approval. This was a very cold fact of the situation. A guy has to decide when it's time to cut his losses. I did. Going way back to 1987, my daughters and I had shared a favorite travel song. It was Kenny Rogers' "The Gambler."

"You got to know when to hold 'em, know when to fold 'em ..."

I knew then it was time to fold 'em. I have replayed this business situation in my mind a thousand times. I still come to the same conclusion. It was an especially grueling time for me, professionally. You might have considered this series of events a major turning point. More than that, it was one of those *defining moments*. Although it took me a while to realize it, this whole scenario crystallized a significant piece of who I am—where I would draw the line, whom I would associate with, and under what circumstances I would continue to have my name aligned with others.

Something else was ingrained in me through this work experience, and I would never want to lose sight of the collateral damage that accompanied my decision. The most painful part was the loss of my relationships with some really good people, especially my former partner. There were also the critics. Two of my peers at least had the guts to chastise me for not staying in the situation, say maybe for another year or so. Quite possibly, another new Managing Director might come along. I simply reminded them that our signature—whether on a proposal, a letter, or a check—must mean something. Under the new structure, my authority had been stripped away. My signature was no longer the final word on virtually any subject of importance within our U.S. operations.

Fortunately, I had never before encountered the type of business practices that I have just described. Nor have I since. But the life lessons it taught are etched into my memory and into my conscience. I will come back to this event a bit later. For now I would just say that I learned that I value my personal standards and sense of ethics more than I value a paycheck or a powerful title and company-furnished luxury automobile. What's more, as a result of how it all played out, I like the guy I see in the mirror each morning when I'm shaving. Defining moments such as this are a blessing.

Before you get the wrong idea about the entire scenario I have just described, let me be clear on one point. I was not a victim. This was not the portrayal of some sort of persecution or other. Mark this: The events of the work place were and still are much of my own making. Sometimes compost happens. As we go deeper into other issues and life aspects that this book is all about, you can be certain that in every case I have some level of personal responsibility. Men, we own our choices, our decisions, our mistakes, and, yes, our shortcomings.

Earlier I said there would always be people who seem to get on your nerves. You know, they just rub you the wrong way. How do you deal with them, especially when you see clearly that they are not about to change?

Here's one approach. Do all you can to destroy or discredit that person. Surprised? Don't be. As a young officer, I had two actual experiences where this was the sincere counsel I received. First, a prominent dentist in my home town, with whom I had a brief chat at the country club one evening, told me in very cold words and with emotionless facial expression, "Sometimes you just have to, you know, squash 'em." The words were accompanied by some gestures, just to drive home the point. He raised one foot, slammed it to the floor, and then ground his heel. You know, squash 'em. Following this brief bit of theatrics, his steely eyes and his cold smirk told me that this was one of his secrets to success. Fortunately, it never became mine.

Fast forward about two years to another approach. As a company commander of some 180 people, I observed that a particular sergeant in my unit was a slacker—all talk and no action. I didn't tolerate his work ethic, and I let him know about it frequently. Before our normal 6 a.m. physical training time one morning, I spotted some very strong, defamatory words that had been spray-painted on our building. The words were directed at me, of course. It didn't take long to discover that this same slacker sergeant was the midnight graffiti king. My company First Sergeant, the senior enlisted man of the unit, offered to (in his words) bring me this guys head on a platter. With a wink of his eye he was really telling me that someone could plant evidence of some serious violation of military law in the sergeant's quarters, so I could then strip him of his rank, income, and long term benefits. Basically, such non-judicial punishment could run him out of the service. Obviously, it never happened. Initially, I dismissed the First Sergeant's suggestion as a joke—maybe even a little test of my integrity. But I sensed in my gut that he was not joking. This was the post-Viet Nam era. Could he, would he, have set this man up for a fall? I wasn't certain. But it did open my eyes to the realities of what co-workers were capable of.

Maybe another possibility for you is to follow this old adage: Keep your friends close, and your enemies closer. The good piece of this as I see it is that you at least keep in close contact and dialog with the other person. The bad news is that your motivation is sinister, and you can never really achieve personal peace in your day to day dealings. In the long run I believe you are the one who suffers most.

Dealing with difficult co-workers takes considerably more work on your part. I wouldn't recommend any of the approaches you've just read. What you have often heard said is true: Take the high road. In order to defeat the part of you that wants to just reach out and strangle this other person that you feel always at odds with, you have to replace your tense feelings with something else, something better. Need a suggestion? Why not act as if this person were your brother or sister? (I am assuming your sibling is not among your regular sources of irritation.) Show the person all the kindness, courtesy, and basic human dignity that you can muster; show it all the time. Armed with this attitude and disposition, you can actually begin to feel better about yourself, not worse. Now, if you're a "man's man," watch this next note. In taking on this respectful attitude, it in no way means you are a wimp. Quite the contrary is true. This warmer disposition is also very different from the idea of patronizing the other person. What it does mean is that you are so self-assured and spiritually strong that you don't have to act or react negatively no matter how offensive the other person has been. In the end, you win. And don't be too surprised if the other person actually fades away from your daily concerns. You may also discover that the other person warms up to you. *Your attitude* made the difference.

I want to share a few final thoughts about work, and I will begin with a comment for men who are already raising a family. As we saw on the second point of the star, family, we have a unique opportunity to do things differently; and hopefully they will be somewhat better than the way we were reared. My concern is that we be thoughtful and cautious about where we look for our role models.

We will encounter plenty of misguided experts out there. Each is driven by his own set of principles, and he or she has been tempered by a particular series of life-changing experiences. And then you have your friends who can be quick to tell you how you should handle such-and-such a decision. This is where you have to be keenly attentive. Allow me to suggest one little test before taking in what others have to say. Ask yourself, "Are they in any way *invested* in the outcome of whatever I decide?" Some folks may have a peripheral knowledge of your current dilemma. But no one knows the facts and circumstances as you do. No one else is tied to the outcome the way you are.

Guys, my summary comment about work boils down to this—encouragement to be your own person. Speaking of role models, shouldn't we also ask ourselves, "What kind am I?" In other words, are we the best dads we can be? That does not imply that we must be the nicest, the friendliest, the most giving, or the most permissive. It is up to us to model our values in all we say and in all we do. Our spouses can so often be a sounding board for work issues. If we're lucky, we can discuss these things without fear or threat. Just remember that our kids are always observing us and learning from us. We can lose sight of this fact all too easily.

I love fireworks. Are you ready for some? Here is my last reflection on work life. While I was in my thirties, as a very young parent, the culturally accepted norm was for the woman to do and have it all—be the best Mom, be a loving and devoted wife, and be the best in her full-time professional career. The advertising slogans seemed to run along the same theme as Helen Reddy's contemporary hit song, "*I am strong, I am invincible, I am woman.*" See where this is going? Let me tell you right now, in plain English, to be able to do all three at the same time—especially to be able to do them well—is *pure fantasy*. Now, I recognize that I am addressing guys with young children. Families whose children are under twelve years old would serve my definition. What is *not* fantasy is that the cost of having it all may be paid in other aspects of our lives. It is a choice we make. But have you calculated the cost in terms of caring for and nurturing your children?

Yes, exceptions do exist. Yes, you may be one of them, especially if you have family nearby to assist you. It is left solely to you to determine the potential impact on your own children. But, allow me this question: Are you really going to know for sure until the kids are much older? The odds are stacked strongly against you if yours is a dual-income, latch-key kid family. Consider also single dads or moms. Their challenges are even more immense as only they know best. My heart goes out to them.

I suppose you won't just take my word for this heightened concern over young kids who do not have a stay-at-home parent. That's okay. But allow me this much. Do take the time to learn the facts for yourself. Seek out credible sources, and read up on day-care kids' development compared to kids who were not raised in a day care environment. Read up on latch-key kids' behavioral issues versus kids who came home to a waiting parent. Check out the differences between kids raised in a boarding school and kids living at home with their natural parents. Really look at the statistics and trends, and then decide if income or your children's nurturing is really important. Finally, I give you full permission to shoot the messenger on this point. It does not negate the message.

Now, dads, if we haven't thought enough about how much time and energy we devote to our work lives, get ready. We have yet to even touch on what we do or where we go after work, on weekends, and during our days off. What do we do within our local communities? That's the next point for a *Star Man* to contemplate.

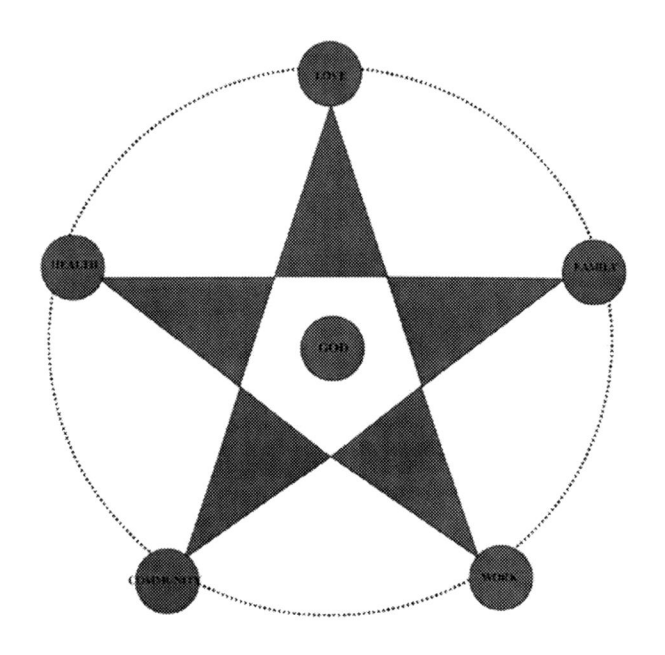

Community

I believe that in all stages of life, the wisest of men will find ways to give something back. It is a simple law of nature that every one of us comprehends. Maybe you've heard this same idea expressed in different quotes such as: "The more you give, the more you receive," "What goes around comes around," and, my personal favorite,"It is more blessed to give than to receive."

We understand this concept, intuitively at least. And it is up to each one of us to figure out how, when, and where we are going to apply it. May I suggest to you that one of the keys to getting started is to just *try something*? So many needs can be found right in our own back yards, and we see reports every day depicting areas of social depravity beyond our normal reach or outside of our national borders. If we look hard enough, I think we will uncover an equal number of groups trying to correct a wide array of social problems. One thing is certain; too few people are actively engaged in these organizations which are trying to make a positive impact. We have to be careful about using absolute language. And yet, in every non-profit community service group I have ever been involved with, I could always identify a core group of people who shouldered the load. It's the old 80–20 rule in action again—20 percent of the people doing 80 percent of the work. So, first, I'd have to say that when you do pick an organization to support, give it your active participation. Don't just show up for the meetings. *Contribute something*.

I have often admired people who have identified that one need or one group that they were passionate about supporting and sticking with it for years on end, often for decades. My personal experience with individual non-profits has been much shorter, but I feel each endeavor was no less rewarding. While it has always been easy to give my time and energies to a group no matter where I have lived, I found that the groups that I saddled up with varied a great deal. Depending on where I lived at the time, on what time constraints I had, on other things my children were involved in, or on what need or opportunity for service I was personally drawn to, my choices ranged from the well-organized to start-ups. Sometimes it mattered to me who else was involved in the group, and normally a social aspect became a spin-off benefit from my participation.

As I think about where I chose to give back, several organizations come to mind. You will recognize most of them: Volunteer Red Cross Water Safety Instructor, The Boy's Club Board (no girls back then), Jaycees, Civic Leagues, Red Cross Homeless Shelters, Vetshouse Inc (transitional housing and support for homeless U.S. military veterans), Habitat for Humanity, and the Juvenile Diabetes Research Foundation. I could go on and on about how much each of these groups has meant to me at different times. But I do not want to lose sight of the main point. It matters little *where* we choose to give of our time and resources. It is *how* or *how well* we serve that is essential.

The real gift of our community service involvement is the one we receive—a deep feeling of personal gratification, if not inner joy which stems from our having made a positive contribution. Do you recall the feeling of adrenaline rush from sports? The equivalent boost we feel from community service is the endorphins which our bodies produce when we help make someone else's life better, less burdened, or more tolerable. In truth, helping others has the boomerang effect of giving us a profound spiritual and emotional uplift.

Let me ask you something here. Suppose we choose to work all the time—say even six days a week. And suppose we save up enough money to go on lots of fun trips, eat very well, and basically live large. With no other place to give some portion of our time and our earnings, how do we ever come to appreciate our blessings and good fortune?

I believe our community needs are so great that ignoring any and all such concerns is simply not an option. And yet, how many men live by such an inwardly focused standard? So, let me go out on a limb again. As a way of broadly categorizing people, I've heard it stated this way: There are three kinds of people—those who know what's going on, those who don't know what's going on, and those who don't know anything is going on!

In the case of giving of ourselves within the community, I am tempted to reduce this to two kinds of men—givers and takers. More often than I care to admit, I have heard men say, "Let the bleeding-hearts take care of the needy," or, "Let someone else give up his time and money. I work hard for mine, and I can barely make ends meet." You might have heard the same message in one of these forms: "Let the rich folks do it," or, "It's the government's job to take care of that problem." No doubt you have listened to many variations of this same theme. Let me be perfectly clear again now. Such are the attitudes of unwise, self-focused souls.

While we are on the subject of being selfishly motivated, I'd like to add a note here about some varying forms of motivation. Let's go back to the point about personal joy in giving back to our community. What I am alluding to is a closer look at the *motivation* behind our giving. First, we will give in whatever forms suit us—time, money, personal contact, comfort, skills—as we are able and willing. We give because we want to, and we do so cheerfully—free from thoughts of doubt or future events. If we truly have a grateful heart, our giving to others will feel as natural and as wholesome as a light summer rain.

Next, as we think about giving back, we should also guard against negative motivations. What do I mean? I have witnessed occasions when men have made a public performance out of making a donation to a favorite non-profit group.

Reckon what moves some men this way. In the business world such instances might be called agendas, or possibly hidden agendas. For example, take the man who joined the local Kiwanis chapter. At his first meeting as a new member, he was quick to get around to everyone and engage them in conversation. He was noticeably adept at turning the talk to what others did for a living, and then he found the right time to make sure to give out a card from his commercial brokerage business. Have you met this man? Is he all about giving, or is he really more concerned about selling something? Now, don't get me wrong. In almost any setting—social, community service, church, or business group—there are frequent opportunities to network with others. These times are usually intentional. Others within the organization are just as eager to network as the first person. Remember when I mentioned givers and takers? I believe the issue here is joining a particular association to be served rather than to serve.

As another brief example, take the man whose job resume includes a laundry list of service organizations that he belongs to. I have always enjoyed probing such listings in the course of interviewing whenever I ran across them. I asked for all kinds of details about what the person did—yes, his *contributions*—and doing so rarely failed to reveal something about his genuine interests. Did he join to add something positive, or did he simply occupy a chair in the meetings? Maybe you'll see this, too, when you are reviewing resumes for whatever group or business you are involved with. Show me a man who would speak with genuine enthusiasm about his volunteer work or organization, and I will show you a man who is *passionate* about the group's mission and success! If you have never given that part of a resume any attention, I heartily recommend it.

At the end of the day, we might all do well to take time and validate our own motivations behind what we do for others. While being certain that it is to benefit others, I would add a final reflection. *Do it whether anyone else ever notices or not.* It is not about personal recognition; it is about giving, sacrificing, loving, sharing, and caring. We will also discover that these actions and attitudes are biblical.

One last aspect of serving the community, I believe, is worth examining. Our service to others is not necessarily about the group or organization. Some of the most beautiful personal sacrifices or gifts to those in need were those done privately. Look around. You may not need to join Big Brothers to do for one select person what that group would do. Must we work within a structure to be of some benefit to a young man in need of a mentor?

Warning: proceed with caution. When I describe the one-on-one, private kind of giving to others, I must say in total honesty that it is not all utopia. When we get involved with someone else, we have to be prepared to share his ups and downs, his good times and bad, and from time to time maybe even his hurtful remarks. Looking back on a few personal examples, I now see such circumstances as a different kind of personal test. If our work life is a test of our ethics and integrity, then the private support or nurturing we give to another person can be, too. At the very least it will test our commitment to that person. Sometimes we have to stop and take a gut check. For example, in caring for an elderly gentleman who lives with dementia, do we really care enough to absorb his occasional verbal attacks without firing back, cutting off the contact, or copping an attitude? If we were in his shoes, might we react the same way at times? Would we be worse?

I truly applaud those who earn service certificates for their many years of working with senior citizens. The Meals on Wheels organization is a wonderful example. These organizations do a tremendous service; and their volunteers are to be praised and thanked every chance we get. Numerous organizations are all about commitment to the community. They are dedicated to the support and care of the people they serve. In plain talk, it is not about the number of people they serve; it is about the people themselves who receive the care.

The concluding part of this message is to just stop, look, listen, and see the needs that are so plentiful and so obvious that we routinely miss them. Historically, men are seldom portrayed as being "sensitive" to others' needs. From my observation, that's a bunch of horse-hockey. Here is what I see: The many men I have encountered will rarely mention their service to others—certainly not as an ice-breaker when meeting someone new. But they are as selfless and socially aware as most professional care providers. There are doers, and there are talkers. These guys are doers.

Who would have thought that giving of ourselves could produce a sense of pain or loss? This kind of hurt came to me in a much unexpected way many years ago. After a couple of good years of frequent contact with a young boy who was under the care of the state foster child program, my family moved hundreds of miles away. After his first visit with us in our new location, we had to decide how to maintain our long-distance relationship or how to cease being his part-time family. His case worker agreed that it was best for him that we make the decision—one way or the other. Our ultimate choice to stop our visits and break off regular contact was extremely difficult. My conversation with him and the case worker was heart breaking—absolutely gut-wrenching.

If you believe that somehow things always work out for good, then you will readily anticipate the final chapter for this young man. As it turned out, a couple of years later we moved back to our former home town. This young man was instantaneously reunited with the family. To this day I am still amazed at how much the relationship with this young man meant to my daughters. Their genuine love and concern for him tells me that he was truly part of our extended family. Despite the period of deep hurt for everyone involved, love, and maybe a dose of divine intervention, took over.

Is some form of community service a point on your star? With needs as overwhelming as they are—locally, domestically, and internationally—how can a guy find time for it all? While I would like to offer up an answer for you, it is totally your call. Just know that you don't have to be the new leader of the pack; you don't always have to go out and hit home runs. Go for some singles—offer your help—and you will surprise yourself at how fast you become an asset to whatever team you choose to join. Either way, you first have to step up to the plate.

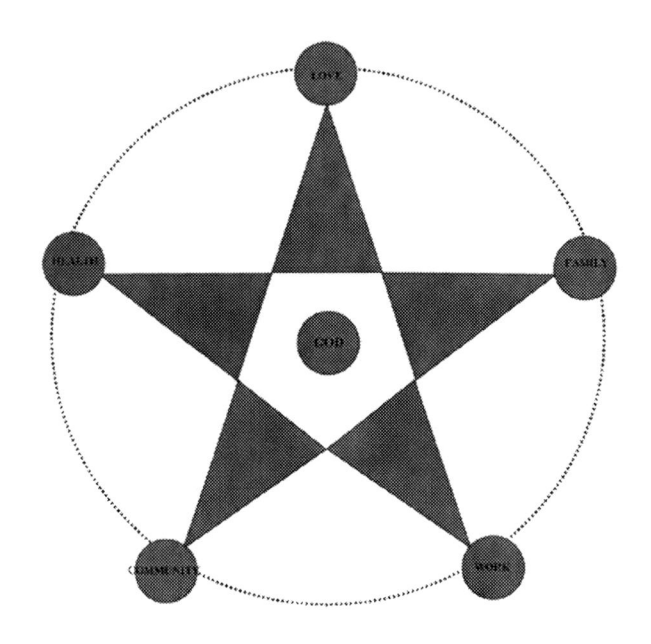

Health

I'm sure it has become obvious to you now that good health is a true blessing. The problem I see is that when we are relatively young—say in our twenties and thirties, even forties—we may not appreciate this fact. At some point—the sooner the better—we have to make changes in our life styles to preserve the health that we enjoy. Unfortunately, some guys will have practiced a bad habit or two long enough to render it an unbreakable ritual which brings about their ultimate demise. Others may suffer terminal illness; they don't have much of a choice in the matter.

This is not news. We have read articles, we have seen the statistics, and we have sensed the complexity of premature death. So, how much more evidence do we need? Notwithstanding all the data that has been published out there on this subject, let me elaborate. Let's start where many of us have been then come to where we are now.

On the physical/medical side, odds are that you were lucky enough to have grown up being fairly active. You were able to enjoy some form of games or sporting activities at an early age. You had your favorites, and you probably adapted well to other kinds of sports or exercises. I had always hoped that my girls would grow up to be lady jocks. And they actually did. One grew up to be a very strong swimmer; the other an excellent fast-pitch softball player. Both were good on snow skis and even better as snowboards came into vogue. At times, I wish I had pulled or pushed them harder to continue with organized sports throughout high school. Even without doing so, they remain physically active and fit—a true blessing.

I want to keep this work authentic and transparent. In that spirit, let me say that if you think my two young adult daughters have been in sync with their Dad on the subject of healthy practices, guess again. In spite of what I have said or done, despite all the lectures I gave or the copies of health magazine articles I dished out to them, I couldn't talk them out of their smoking habit. If you're a dad, you know I'm going to get an earful when my daughters get a hold of this book! But it does not change the fact that we have seen several classic cases where this vice became a crippler if not a killer in the lives of our family members and close personal friends. My grandfather loved his Phillies cigars and his Mail Pouch chewing tobacco. I am convinced these products were root causes of his death from cancer of the tongue and mouth. So, if this comment feels like personal admonishment to you, let me ask: What are you waiting for? It is likely that your spouse, your significant other, your parent, or someone else who cares about you, has already drilled you with similar pleadings. I will say it again on his or her behalf. Do you really need to bring serious health problems on yourself? In today's language, maybe all we have to say is, "Hello-o-o-o-o; anyone home?"

I can't stress enough how important it is to take care of our own bodies. Some kind of physical exercise done regularly is the only way to go. Not one of us is able to know his future or when his time is up. The simple question is this: "Would you rather tempt fate or do something pro-active to improve your chances for longevity?" It's up to you to find the time and the methods that work best for you. The key is to do *something*.

At one time or another we are all going to experience some form of medical or physical challenge. So, I suppose you could argue that until that happens why not go for all the gusto you possibly can. Right? Not right! I believe it is precisely when your ailments and especially serious illnesses start compounding one on top of another that you are most at risk. Quite often these health concerns are life changing, or permanent, or terminal. Here again, I would not expect you to take my word for it. Just go online and Google the phrase "major health issues." The result at the time of this writing is some 136,000,000 hits. The astronomical number of articles and links found there may enlighten you, but allow me to boil it down a bit by sharing a couple of examples that hit close to home.

My personal witness on this issue is a series of blessings. When I was quite young my parents both smoked a little bit, and drank even less. They really never did either one in excess or for any length of time. Though I tested these things for myself—first as a rite of passage as a teenager and then as a college student who was finally out from under parental controls—neither habit became much of a factor in my life. As for behaviors I would not deny having had a few senseless blow-outs involving alcohol. But that was pretty much it. On the medical side, events went a bit differently.

Though I couldn't even imagine it at the time, I now look back on severe knee injuries as blessings. You see, I was eighteen. Coming out of high school, and fairly trim, I thought I was in good shape—darn good actually. I was an athlete who also happened to have a halfway decent scholastic record. When damaged knees literally stripped away most of my physical strength, I had to work extra hard to regain my self-esteem. I battled with a new and unfamiliar erosion of inner confidence. It took years to rebuild. Without a doubt, making it through college and actually graduating felt like a major accomplishment. The chinks in my physical armor were still there, and I would deal with them all my life.

So, what if I were prone to smoking or drinking during these years? Wouldn't this turn of events have been a ready excuse to do more of it and without a doubt to do it to my own detriment? The fact is, with just one drunken episode, I could have been thrown out of school. It happened to some of the guys. They called it *bringing discredit upon the Corps of Cadets*. Let me come back to this period in the final chapters. Right here, I want to acquaint you with a person who has sharpened my understanding of how one deals with truly critical health obstacles. She teaches me something about this almost every day, as she is my soul-mate.

My wife of over fifteen years is what I would consider a medical success story. While she downplays the daily effect of her disease, I continue to marvel at her positive outlook. Through her story, let me offer you some insights from the time when I was just getting to know her and then loving her for who she is. For her, it began at the tender age of thirteen with the onset of Type I (insulin dependent) diabetes. The simple and awesome fact is that for my wife, *every day is a gift*.

Every day as she wakes up, and every night as she retires, she thanks God just to still be alive. I suppose I could develop an entire chapter on how she arrived at such a terrific perspective. Here is an abbreviated rendition of how health concerns have shaped her world:

- In doing her graduate studies, she researched the long term impact of juvenile-onset, Type I diabetes for her master's thesis.
- All research at that time concluded (and so did she) that she would be dead by the age of forty. Even in the early nineteen eighties, regular exercise and proper eating habits were known to have positive effects on longevity. But ultimate failure of certain critical body organs was a given.
- She has developed an acute zest for life.
- She has an appreciation for the profoundly simple things that day to day living offers each of us if we choose to see them.
- She knows how fragile her life can be at times, and she knows intimately—from her nursing profession—how detrimental a person's poor heath habits can be, not to mention how devastating serious diseases or illnesses can be to a person's quality of life. The effects of any serious medical condition are felt by those who are ill, and they tend to be shared by their loved ones.
- From personal experience and exposure, she has a profound awareness of suffering—of physical pain and emotional heartache.

Such a depth of understanding cannot be taught. By sharing this background with you as information, I would hope that it gives you greater insight into the importance of good health. How you react to a story like hers is up to you. But let me add one last note. Chances are good that you know someone with a long term disability or with a severe illness. What new light would he or she shed for you on the issue of individual health if you took the time to just sit and listen to that friend?

In still another way, we men can literally drive ourselves into poor health. We can allow pressures at home or at work, conflicting needs, doubts, and fears to dominate our daily lives. Are you with me? These influences can become big-time stresses or worries at best and depression or critical dysfunction at worst. The larger question I would like to address is: Whoever said that expressing feelings is not a *guy thing*?

First, let me remind you here and now that men need an outlet! We may have widely varying saturation points, but each of us has a limit to the level of pressures or fears we can tolerate. I wrote earlier about many of the effects of divorce on family life. I guarantee you this feeling of loss—especially of my full time status with the children—was true for me. Unfortunately, my daughters were on the receiving end of several mind games back then. Among the most difficult for me to ever understand was when they were threatened by my former spouse in words to this effect: "If you don't straighten up and do as your told, I'm going to send you away to live with your father." To this day, I can't stress enough how that must have driven a mental wedge between my children and me—not to mention how it got under my skin. The saddest day for any man is when he can't be the hero to his own children. When I finally got wind of this comment to my daughters, you can't imagine how badly I needed an outlet!

Such parental control games are enough to make a grown man cry. And I did. Often. Two divorced adults fell into the trap of displaying some really bad behavior. Some twenty years later, I would like to think the kids survived all that stuff. Maybe they did. Time will tell. So long as they avoid playing out any of those old tapes for themselves, they will continue to grow in their emotional health as well as the physical.

Remember now, this is still guy talk—man to man. What follows may sound a little like psychology. I do not claim any such professional pedigree. What I will draw upon is a decade or so of experience in counseling, plus a few years as a certified mediator. I want to describe an area which I believe carries the potential of being emotionally unhealthy. What if it were your job as the child to do *only* as your father and mother wanted you to do, to the extent that not behaving as prescribed meant the possibility of being sent away? Think about that image. How would you ever feel unconditional love and family support? As a young child, what else would you do? Now, add to this early insecurity another recurring message you received as an adolescent: "What you did was okay, but it wasn't good enough." As you got older, the stakes got much higher. Do thus and so in this manner, or we will cut you out of your inheritance. These are precisely the types of messages that are devastating to a man's emotional well-being. Having witnessed a guy who lived in this exact situation, let me state clearly—there is no amount of money that is worth a man giving up who he is, who he wants to be, or what he chooses to believe. Live and work for your own dreams—your own goals. *You* will have accomplished these things, and then some. *You* will have achieved a greater degree of confidence and self-esteem than you ever thought possible. And, to bring it full circle, what could be better for your own mental health?

Also on the emotional side of healthy living, I would like to swing back to what I said concerning the first point for a *Star Man*. You will do well if you can find a good soul-mate. Coupled with a supportive mate, you must know what you believe in and what or whom you have faith in to develop a firm foundation. A best friend—the kind who may often disagree with you or challenge you—is also invaluable. It's when you hit tough times that you call on your best allies and on your personal belief system to support you. You've probably already found that by *being there* for someone else, he in turn wants to be there for you. I can't determine who said it first, but I love the old quote, "To have a good friend, be one." If you already have a handle on this universal truism, I congratulate you. You are a fortunate man, and your friends are fortunate.

Even though time and distance separate us, my two brothers and I can always rely on each other the same way. It is the kind of bond that lasts forever. If there is not a blood brother in your life, someone whom you would consider your best friend or mentor can be your next best ally.

Strange and atypical as it may seem, I find that guys are becoming more and more willing to talk to each other about their feelings. Yeah, really! I have encountered men engaged in matter-of-fact dialog regarding their deepest feelings, fears, concerns, weaknesses, failures, acts of utter stupidity, and a whole host of personal subjects. Look around a little. Guys can most often be found doing this in small groups—usually two to four people. They keep it small, so they can keep it real. The smaller the group, it seems, the more likely they will dig into personal issues. And they never have to wake up the next day and read about it in the local gossip column a week later. They also hold each other accountable to do the right thing. Guys who talk with each other regularly will encourage one another to follow through on a change planned or a promise made. It is in this small group setting that men don't judge one another. They are listened to.

Most women seem more adept than men at forming close relationships within their gender. Guys just have a gene deficiency in this area. As a group, women appear to find it easier to express their innermost feelings openly. But, not having been welcomed into any women's talk circles recently, I rely on female friends and neighbors for support of my assertion. From my admittedly narrow sample, I conclude that their discussions seldom turn to bold challenges or prescriptions for definitive corrective action. I, for one, sure can't sit through lengthy dialog without some hard-line, straight-forward, guy feedback. I want someone to take me to task on my thought process or my attitude. Otherwise, it's not likely I'll get any benefit out of the time invested. It's a guy thing.

In truth, I spent too many years surrounding myself with those whom I knew in advance to have held similar outlooks or beliefs. I believe it is in expressing our views—or defending them—which we grow emotionally. We all recognize that there are times when it helps just to vent. Some would describe it as cutting loose. But a couple of guys who can hold confidences, and who are willing to fire back at me, and I them, now that's a plus! Who do you know that could become this type of brother to you? How fortunate for you if you are already part of such a group. A couple of personal teammates have a unique way of keeping a guy on track.

In discussing this whole point about our physical and mental health, I would encourage you to appreciate the importance of taking good care of yourselves—in every sense of the word. I firmly believe that when we don't care well enough for ourselves, we sacrifice at least a portion of the positive impact we can have on others.

Allow me one final observation here about personal communications and confidences. Some of my best occasions for sanity checks are when my wife and I take evening bike rides, walks, or dog walks. These moments are just as mentally centering as they are physically healthy. They also provide one of the best means for us to stay emotionally connected. The main thing here is just to find out what works for you—something you can stick with and do regularly.

For your health's sake, make time to enjoy Mother Nature. As a kid growing up, it was trips to the country and to the lake that got me hooked. In the country meant riding out to small communities in western Pennsylvania—some twenty to thirty miles outside of Pittsburgh—where a lot of my cousins lived. This region of rural communities was also the area where my Dad grew up—you guessed it—on a farm. I always felt a sense of freedom there. Out in the country, my brothers and I were exposed to Mother Nature at her finest. We learned of such things as: the smell of fresh air, crystal clear (and cold) streams, salamanders, snakes, lizards, deer flies, frogs, baling hay, crops in fields, shooting guns, riding tractors, farm tools and machinery, big trucks, real country kitchens, real country cooking, down-to-earth people, what "laid-back" meant, pitch-black nights, star-filled skies, campouts (versus sleep-overs), acting silly without getting in trouble, real fires and fireplaces, tree varieties, fishing, going "number one" outside (now there's a symbol of real freedom for a man!), yelling at the top of your lungs and nobody cares, wild animals, farm animals, horses, riding bare-back, riding without a bridle, swimming in a pond, loud echoes in the woods even though all you did was step on some twigs and leaves, trees acting as umbrellas, tadpoles, wild berries and roots you can eat, crab apples, where milk and cheese and eggs really come from, and insects you've never seen before or even heard of. My list could go on, but you are already thinking of many of your own.

I look back on a scenic and at the same time rustic place from my young adult life also. The town and area was called Grand Isle, Vermont. I have always felt that was a cool name. It was a cool place too, literally speaking; most of the year it was down right frigid. It was an area that was quite new for me, too, as it was for my infant daughters. And, if you ever wanted to experience some really cold water, this was the place. The ice-cold, churning waves of Lake Champlain offer about the toughest conditions I had ever known, especially during the annual task of launching the floating dock in the early spring. But, our summers were filled with some of the warmest images I may ever appreciate. I can still draw from a soul-full of colorful mental pictures.

For instance, I close my eyes and envision these: boiling lobsters for the Sunday cookout, fishing from shore or from the boat, little girls' tangled lines, kids sitting upright in the boat while fast asleep and still clinging onto the fishing rod, crisp air and mist blowing across my face, fires at night and early morning (yes, even in summer), neat hiding places, compost, rustic tools from the nineteenth century, real country stores and farmer's markets, home-made everything on the

Fourth of July (including everything used in the local parade), trees that grow sideways out of rough cliffs and overhangs, floating docks, drive-in movies, fireworks reflecting off the lake, and breath-taking sunsets. I wonder how many natural sensations such as these you can recall. Have you seen them lately?

When it comes to a man's health benefits of communing with nature, I hardly know where to begin. The best picture I can offer you is through a few memorable moments.

In the late eighties and early nineties, things were extremely tight for us financially. So we found ourselves very fortunate to be able to escape the congestion of a condominium complex. We would flee to the trails within our local state park in Eastern Pennsylvania. It was only a ten-minute bike ride from our front door, but in the park and the bordering farmlands, we found joy in the simple things. And they carried us a long way. It was peaceful. In effect, we had returned to *the country*. Babbling brooks fed the main stream. Chipmunks and squirrels played. Geese and ducks gazed back at us, then flew low overhead and mocked our inability to fly with their loud and continuous squawks. It was perfect. And it was soothing. We talked a lot as we ambled through these woods. And we listened—occasionally to each other, of course—but also to Mother Nature. It was in this relatively little park that we found restoration for our spirit and our sense of well being. We found tranquility. What a great word that is—tranquility. The word even *sounds* like the calming effect that it imparts.

A flashback: I was about eight years old. I had achieved the age of young manhood—old enough to join the men at a small hunting cabin somewhere in the Blue Ridge Mountains. My Uncle Bob and some of his buddies had a hunting cabin there. My Dad and I went there for a few days one summer. Maybe we stayed a week. All I know for certain is that I didn't want to return home. The trip was full of *men-folk* lessons, such as how men practiced their pistol and shotgun shooting, how they stayed up late till the kids were asleep (they thought), how they played cards and drank a bit telling stories all the while. Here was a glimpse at the whole idea of guys being guys—the natural beauty of the woods around us, combined with the air of feeling relaxed and comfortable. I later understood this as camaraderie, fellowship, and brotherhood. These impressions are indelibly etched into my mind. They are a part of who I am.

Fast-forward sixteen years or so. Skiing in the German/Austrian border area was yet another natural high. The final set of lifts attained such heights that we stood at the top of the mountain and peered down into the clouds. We stood at an altitude well above them. As they shifted and drifted, the clouds gave brief glimpses of tiny clusters of dots—the villages—down below. The runs started above the highest treetops. We peered down on a panorama of other mountain tops. In certain spots along the trail, we saw nothing but mountaintops in all directions. With the exception of the villages, as far as I could possibly see, it was the same view of uninhabitable, unspoiled, rugged, snow-capped mountains.

Fast-forward again, this time to the Garden of the Gods in Colorado. I had the pleasure of riding through there one summer on a guided horseback tour. Man, was it ever hot! One of the locals said the heat wasn't so bad since the humidity was so low. I wasn't buying it. Besides, I'm sure he stole that line from someone in Arizona. But neither of the two immediate factors—the expressionless guide and the oppressive heat—detracted from the experience. This western area of America was another instance of nature showing its own version of rugged beauty and towering rock formations. I saw divine creativity in the rock strata, in the plant life, and in the seemingly endless trail of unique land patterns and fissures. Who knew the landscape produced so many kinds of cacti? There was no substitute for employing all six senses and for experiencing such a place in person.

The list of nature's incredible sites is endless. Heading my list of final examples, the Grand Canyon must also be included among our most natural beauties. We couldn't fly over all of it on a two-hour, fixed-wing aircraft tour. And what about the whole world under water? Scuba in the Florida Keys, Cancun, Greece, or any similar destination, opens up a whole new world—fish and plant life of all sizes, shapes, and colors of a rainbow. Back at Lake Champlain, Vermont, the submerged landings for the old Grand Isle Ferry were hauntingly dark at the bottom, and yet it turned gorgeous when a ray of sunlight beamed through every now and then. This was a massive structure formed by huge trees and boulders—a perpetual witness to the talented engineers of the eighteen hundreds and to their creative use of natural materials.

If you are the outdoor type, then chances are good you also have an appreciation of what it means for a guy to be physically fit. Surely we can understand that personal fitness has its place for us. And we can see to it that we do something to take care of ourselves. To me, this aspect has equal value to other areas we have considered so far. I am not one to overemphasize the importance of health and nature in a man's life, but I hold it up to you as the fifth point of a man's quest for balance.

What we have yet to examine is the center of the star, the hub from which all of the spokes extend outward and are supported. I believe that is where a *Star Man* finds his greatest source of strength, courage, and love—from a personal relationship with his God.

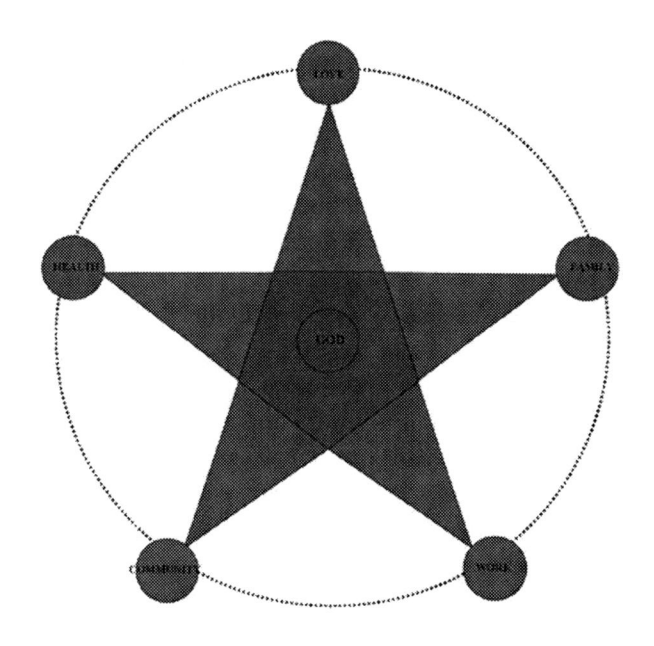

God

I believe that in all aspects of our lives God is at the center. Whether we choose to recognize this fact, or whether we choose to ignore it, is in itself a God-given choice. But, amazingly, by our merely seeking to discern who God is for us, or what God means to us, we find Him. We also discover that He has always been there. More than that, we come to realize that God has always been reaching out to us and waiting for us to respond. Somewhere in this last statement, I believe, is God's ultimate message for each of us personally. God meets us where we are—in our home life or in our daily work. It has nothing to do with where we think we need to be before God will reveal Himself to us. Equipped with this new-found knowledge of God, we come to the most awesome realization of all—that we don't *earn* God's care. As we develop a relationship with Him, we cultivate a new sense of living life His way. All this comes from God's grace.

It would be tempting to open and close this section of my message to you right here—tempting, but of no value without offering some real world experiences—my *evidence* if you will. As I look back over each of the five points on our star, I see the direct influences that God has had and continues to have in my life. I am just one guy among hundreds of millions. But God cares about me. And He cares about you, too. So, where was God revealed? Let's take another look.

As kids, I believe my brothers and I were among the blessed ones. We grew up in a family that believed in God and we tried to live by the lessons we learned from church participation. Our grandparents, as I have described for you earlier, were rock-solid spiritual leaders and nurturers among all of us kids; and I have no doubt that this spilled over to include most of our aunts, uncles, and cousins. My own parents were no less effective in giving us this type of spiritual foundation. We were blessed in so many ways that we couldn't fully appreciate it until our teenage or young adult years. Typical of our age group, our understanding of this truth came into our consciousness through interaction with others, especially those who were noticeably less fortunate than ourselves. Even now the richness of what our family gave us is still unfolding. And it is a spine-tingling feeling every time my mind is drawn back into those earlier days. It is as though I am connecting with my ancestors—especially those now deceased—all over again in vivid pictures and memory flashes. This marvel often feels similar to a sensation of déjà vu. It evokes a sense of humility as well. You see, it is now humbling to recognize how often I deviated from their examples as a parent. Luckily, the story isn't over yet, and I still consider my parental role as a work in process.

Why is faith such a big deal?

For starters, by now you have met plenty of men who have never been exposed to formal religious teaching or practice of any kind. Maybe that describes you. They haven't thought much about—much less talked about—God or a Supreme Being. They may believe there is no God, or they may not know what to believe. This is one area where I can say with absolute confidence, *I know for sure*. How often does a man get to say that?

Though I had gone through several periods of rejecting my own spiritual base, I always knew better somewhere deep down. Even though, at times, it felt as if I were just going through the motions in my religious practice and doing the Sunday church thing, I knew. I was absolutely certain that God not only exists, but also that His will or His direction always prevails no matter how stubborn I get. And, I have demonstrated beyond any doubt that I could get plenty stubborn—especially when it came to protecting my own personal goals or ambitions. Any time I needed a reminder of my own bull-headedness, I had only to watch and listen to my daughters; they reflect this trait frequently.

With my daughters in mind, let me share something here. I tried very hard to show them that God, in general—in our case Christianity, in particular—was very important. I always believed in a life of faith as being central in our learning. But it sure seems we didn't live it very well or follow through as we should have. For my own part, being raised in the Protestant church, I encountered a few stumbling blocks in trying to rear the girls in the Catholic Church tradition. I rationalized that it is all one God. Christian is Christian. No big deal. Besides, I was confident in my self-proclaimed maturity and in my ability to improve on things in my own family compared to the way I was brought up. I was confident, but my disposition sure did resemble pride. I could not imagine why I needed to rack my brain on something so easy to figure out. I was self-assured, and I was wrong.

Unfortunately, as time went on, and as I came to learn more about religion, I grew increasingly uncomfortable. Not having converted to Catholicism for example, I was not permitted to receive communion. As one Christian in the company of others, I interpreted this situation as a form of exclusion. And it was a constant reminder—every Sunday. But the simple fact was, this was *my* choice (did I mention I was stubborn?). Despite this thought that boiled beneath the surface, I didn't let this mental reservation become a source of family turbulence. In fact, as a family we did plenty of *church things* together. But, looking back on that time period, it seems my spouse and I lacked a truly unified spirit. We didn't really claim or demonstrate the genuine joy and deep conviction that our faith offered us. Incidentally, the girls went to the *right* (parochial) school as long as we could keep them there. We supported the school and the church which was affiliated with it. Still, it seems we took care of such things as though we were on autopilot.

A man lives and develops his character by the choices he makes. None of us is exempt. And it must be another one of those guy things not to be as observant at home as we should be. For me, it held true as I look back and see there were some early indications that we weren't following through very well on the spiritual upbringing front. What I would say to you now is to watch out for words like *always* and *never*. These are tell-tale signals in the household vocabulary. As a young family, we always said grace when family or friends were over. We never said grace when it was just us two parents at the table. We always said bedtime prayers with our daughters. We never said a prayer together, just us two parents at home before turning in for the night.

So, for us, God was in our home, but He was treated more as a guest than as a resident and constant guide. We didn't live as though God was allowed to be our daily source of love and confidence. As you think about what you believe, with your personal experience at home being your frame of reference, I encourage you to dig back into the Bible for yourself. I guarantee you will find your true beliefs and your true values there. Look there *first*.

Right here is where I would fully expect you to raise all sorts of flags concerning faith. You are thinking to yourself, "What about other religions? What about the God—without Jesus—that our Native Americans believe in, or Buddhism, or Islam? Are they all *wrong*?" As a layman and a lay pastor, I confess that this is an area that I have wrestled with quite often. I think it is both proper and necessary to respect all forms of religion which are based on principles of love and brotherhood. At the same time, I believe that the true God is the God who has been revealed to us all in the Holy Bible. I believe we can and must openly reject any form of extremism that is based on hate, yet claims a religious foundation. As I have already presented in different ways, I believe in God, in Jesus the Christ, and in the power of the Holy Spirit. How do you answer this question for yourself? At some point, we all have to make a decision concerning our beliefs. We must decide who Jesus was and is.

As I have said from the very beginning, not much of what is said here can have any real meaning without life examples. Once again, I rely upon personal experiences. As I do, keep in mind this is only one man's background shaped by Judeo-Christian values.

From the time my kids could read, I know that they read the Bible. They continued doing so until probably the age of twelve or thirteen. The question I have often asked them as twenty-plus year olds is if they have read or studied the Bible now that they have become young adults. Have they compared all of their new learning and life experience as young adults against their childhood memory of what they remember from the Bible? If not, can they really say they know what the Bible says?

I grew up with biblical lessons and exposure right through high school. These fundamental teachings followed me into college. It wasn't until the mid-eighties—after my divorce and all of the pain, guilt, emotional ups and downs, and trials that come with it—that I started reading the Bible again.

Now, if you're a divorced guy, or if you have experienced the loss of love, you know full well that my return to reading the Scriptures did not happen overnight. No one wakes up the next morning having been healed. To remain perfectly honest, I must admit that this transition, this return to my personal basic beliefs, took time. Here is what I mean: For a good four months, post-divorce, I definitely found ways to escape the constant feelings of guilt or failure. Are you familiar with the phrase, "burning the candle at both ends?" Well, I sure did; I put the term into practical application, too. Staying out late, new-found freedom on weekends, trying a variety of new drinks, new woman friends, the whole scene, was a complete diversion from the mucked-up mess I was in. These getaways felt really good, too—for a while.

Then late one Saturday night, I vividly recall passing a local church. It was the same denomination I grew up with as a teenager. I turned around, flashed my bright beams on the marquee out front, jotted down the service times, and went in later that morning. I was instantly impressed at how friendly everyone was that day and at how comfortable I felt throughout the service. They even sang one of my favorite hymns that morning, *How Great Thou Art*. I knew then and there that I would come back. Actually, I *was* back, and for a long time. Was this another one of those major, personal turning points? Indeed it was; this was another one of those *defining moments*. Was God involved? Without question.

When I mentioned earlier about picking up the Bible again, this is how it went. Once I got back into the practice of participating in church life, I recognized many of the verses. But I got to a point where many things I had read before in the Bible said new and more profound things to me this time around—yet another breakthrough in understanding how the Bible remains timeless. Here was one more: While concentrating on not being so down about a particular situation, I was also amazed at how biblical messages would jump right off the page at me even when I had just opened the Bible at random. This phenomenon had become a frequent occurrence. When reading words of Scripture from the difficult perspective of pain or personal challenge, I believe there is comfort if not genuine guidance to be found. Some say this is a chance occurrence. I think otherwise; I see God in action.

Just by reading the Bible a couple chapters at a time, I discovered a new morning ritual. It was usually the Bible and coffee on the back deck. This quiet time enabled me to read the Bible a couple times through in the course of a few years. I am not talking about how fast a person can read; it is about reading and reflecting in order to grasp the meaning. I can't tell you how often, but it is in the hundreds, when something very powerful happened during my reading time. Let me share one.

It is no coincidence that Bible passages of a particular day's sequential reading came at the precise time I was struggling with a key issue. Picture this: A co-worker with whom I had frequent contact was naturally irritable, didn't smile much, and didn't seem to want to work with me in any way. Remember that one person who we just can't seem to work well with? It so happens that one morning after a series of rather obvious snubs from this person, the passage I had read that morning gave me the clear instruction I needed; it said I was to pray for this person. Pray for him? Are you kidding me? Since I didn't care for this person very much, praying for him seemed totally unreasonable. So, okay, I prayed for him.

You can probably guess what happened next. Within a few days, for no apparent reason, this person started talking to me in civil tones. No pot-shots. No sarcastic quips. He even talked a little about his family, his background, and his personal goals. Did my praying for this man change him? Maybe so. Did it change the way I looked at him, the way I talked to him, or the mannerisms and non-verbals that accompanied my speech? I'd have to say yes, it did. I am absolutely certain that what changed was *my attitude* toward him, enough so for him to take note and to respond with more openness toward me. What power! Regardless if my prayers actually inspired change in him, or in me, or both of us, the point here is about the act of prayer. *Praying works.*

Whether or not you think much about it, prayer power is no surprise to you. You said a prayer any time you said, "Please God, just let me get through this_____." You fill in the blanks. This test when you were in school, this personal crisis, this meeting with your boss, or this medical condition, may have been your personal prayer concern. For as long as we have problems and trials, we will say prayers.

Have you have ever been thinking about someone for a while, then, out of nowhere, the person calls you for no specific reason? Have you considered that this may have been a form of silent prayer? I am certainly not up to speed on the latest medical research concerning mind power. But I am convinced that we have far more human capacity that has yet to be discovered and utilized. If strong mental thoughts of another person can actually produce action on his part, doesn't that suggest fervent prayer works at least as well? I like to think of prayer as sending out personal radio waves—microwaves through the air—where they are both sent out and returned. I believe that's how prayer works.

When you dig into God's role in your life, and really grasp the idea of Father, Son, and Holy Spirit, do you take any special notice of the latter? I believe the Holy Spirit works in many ways and is significant in all we do. I don't know the words to capture His essence. But I do know for sure that a very powerful Holy Spirit is at work in your life and in mine. It is as though we truly possess a sixth sense. If we are open to the Spirit, then the Spirit will find us right where we are. We will feel and know His presence. I must also say that we have to make room in all of our busy-ness for this to happen. One of the keys is to find quiet times for ourselves—times long enough and frequent enough for us to be able to listen.

Let me come back now to the point about men who have had little or no background in religious teachings. You might be surprised to know that many of those people can be found at church and church-related functions. Church pews today are filled with them. They are asking lots of insightful questions and looking in earnest for answers. Beyond that, they are finding spiritual nourishment in the Bible and what it teaches. So, whether or not a guy was brought up in these teachings, he will benefit from continued discovery of these spiritual matters. But he must take the first step. Whether from churched or un-churched backgrounds, I promise that guys have a great deal in common. We are all prone to getting way off center from time to time. We are all seekers of something greater than ourselves.

Even as I began to write on this subject, I received a new revelation. It occurred to me that a man may find intrigue in the different cultures and world religions that he hears about. New television broadcasts and magazine articles on the subject are popping up every month. Go to Yahoo on the topic of God, and you will be amazed at the hundreds of millions of hits you will uncover—over 428,000,000 of them! It is mind-boggling. No way that a guy can process so much raw information. Click on the key word Christianity and you can select from over 53,000,000 sites. At best, we might latch onto one or two major links and contrast them with our own experiences. We could compare the contents against our individual background knowledge—what we recall from school, family, or work. I have long preferred, and may I recommend to you, weighing such things against the most widely used resource of all time—the Bible. As I said before, I would encourage every man to check out what the Bible has to say. It is not a man's level of experience that is so important. What means more is his willingness to be continually instructed by what the Good Book reveals to him.

For my part, I recall living this out in reverse order. Prior to and leading into our confirmation as members of the church, my group of fellow twelve year olds learned about other world religions. Periodically, we would revisit world religions through my senior high school years. By age seventeen, I figured I truly had heard and read enough to choose Christianity.

To a greater extent, I was really just acting, repeating, and responding according to the beliefs of my peers and my relatives, and especially my parents. True statement. Even so, through all sorts of exposure to other cultures, I now remain confident in my Christian beliefs. I feel fortunate to have witnessed a variety of religious practices and rituals through personal travels in over fifty countries. So, as you search and research, I commend the Bible to your reading and study. I guarantee you will often be surprised by the wisdom and truth found there. Though you may have read some of it years ago, try doing so again. Given your life experiences since the last time you may have read from the Good Book, you may feel as though you are reading many of its passages for the first time.

The basis of my writing to you is reduced to this simple point—that God is the center of the star; He is at the center of all that a man does. God seeks a personal relationship with us all. But, He will never demand it or force His desires on you or me, though He obviously *could*.

You have seen the beauty of our natural environment. Has it never crossed your mind that you might be seeing small pieces of the face of God in that splendor? I have felt the presence of God in nature enough to give me a chill. Despite all of the jokes to the contrary, guys are very intuitive. And yes, we have a sensitive side. I still find inspiration and peace in just placing myself in one of God's natural settings. Come join me on the back deck or the front porch at 5:30 am—me on mine and you on yours. Sit quietly. Close your eyes periodically, and absorb His simple and natural gifts that such a moment offers. Or, watch as the eastern sky opens and you are slowly warmed by the sun. God is in that moment. He created it.

God also gave men freedom of choice, which means we will run into troubles periodically. Although we may not realize it at the time, God is at work with us when we are facing hardships, frustrations, fears, or doubts. Let me repeat the first part of that statement—*though we may not realize it at the time*.

Sometimes it seems we create our own troubles, and then we act surprised by the consequences. And sometimes bad stuff just happens. As I indicated earlier, compost happens! What matters most is how we react or respond. At that precise moment of trouble, it is extremely difficult to wait patiently for the good aspect of the situation to reveal itself. We tend to bemoan the fact that things aren't happening as fast as we need them to. I believe these are the moments in which we are being tested. That is God's way. These are precisely the times when a guy has to have faith, and he has to trust that God's plan will be revealed. It will be; and it will be a good one.

I've heard over and over again that talking about such things is not what guys do. To that I reply, "Rubbish." Patrick Morley, author of the best-seller *The Man in the Mirror*, and President of Man in the Mirror, a non-profit organization that helps men discover meaning and purpose, would argue that men have been discussing their personal issues or trials with each other for decades! In his more recent work, *Seven Seasons of the Man in the Mirror*, Morley points out that men have always wanted their lives to count in their families and in their work; men also wanted some level of financial success. But, Morley concludes, men want their lives to count for God, too! Men—real men with real concerns—are talking together all over the country.

Let's face it, our fathers and grandfathers would seldom if ever talk about what deep fears or anxieties they had. This held true especially when it came to worries about their jobs. And they definitely would not talk to their sons and grandsons about reading men's magazines or an obsession with gambling. If they were to embarrass the family, break the law, have an extra-marital affair, or hit the booze every night, would they admit such things? Of course not. These social indiscretions would never be discussed. I'm not talking here about the ones who did any of these things openly, or those who were found out. I refer to men who were into any form of vice which they were able to conceal.

Fortunately, my own Dad didn't have any major skeletons in his closet. Good man that he is, he would also make certain that family matters remained the private domain of our family members only. He wrote a lot of business reports in his career. But, I'm betting he would never consider writing—much less *publishing*—some of the things I have expressed in these chapters.

Guys, it's a new day. And we are waking up to it. Years ago, I thought I was the only man on the planet who refused to expose his own personal weaknesses and problems. I was convinced that other guys did not have the same feelings I did. Then I started reading some inspirational works and several self-help books. (One was entitled *"How to Get Control of Your Time and Your Life"* by Alan Lakein. It was a skinny little book, easy enough to follow, but I just couldn't find the time to read it!) When I actually picked up a copy of *The Man in the Mirror*, soon I met up with two other guys who had also read Morley's book. We chatted a bit; then we started having breakfast together once a week. We talked about surface issues for a while—you know—sports, general concerns about business, or our kids' activities. After a few weeks, the topics of conversation got a little more personal. Having developed mutual trust as friends and confidants, we got to know the real man behind the man that everyone else saw. We had families to share things with, and that was wholesome. But we also found in each other a well-spring of support, a personal sounding board, and a tight circle of guys who would call each other to task if we were reacting inappropriately to a situation or just plain being stupid.

Our open dialog was never a breach of the husband-wife bond. It was simple talk, void of any kind of judgment and complete with honest feedback from a man's perspective. Sure, a man must be careful in his selection of whom to trust. Yes, a man must be open and honest with his brothers. Definitely, a man would only want to create such a team with guys he respects. This small band of brothers formed a real network in the true sense of the word. Little did we know it would become a source of strength, even a means of perseverance when times were the toughest. Today, some fifteen years later, I find myself in a new city with new friends and neighbors. And I now count it a blessing to be part of a four-man group whose purpose is to support, challenge, and encourage one another. Who are your brothers?

We have gone all around the points on the star. At every point, I have tried to offer personal testimony as to why I think each of these aspects of daily life is worthy of a man's attention. More than that, I believe these points offer men two valuable insights—balance and perspective. By now, you should also have no doubt as to where I see the role of faith and God in our lives. Taken individually, each of these areas can be examined, and we can come up with our own ideas for individual action. That remains my sincere hope. On any given day, we can touch some or all of these areas of daily living. We can do so without being aware of it; men are creatures of habit. However, I submit to you that we are better served by having a personal plan and purpose.

I am more convinced than ever before that each point of our star represents a vital aspect of a fulfilling life. I also believe faith and God form the necessary focal point in all that we do. If you have ever read the autobiographies of some of our greatest United States Presidents, names you know—Washington, Lincoln, Truman—you learned that each of these men worked through and endured extremely difficult events in his life and in world history. All of that is well documented. You would also encounter many stories from their youth or from their early careers which provided a foundation for their later, weightier decisions. These were truly great men. I am inspired by their backgrounds.

Not so well known, but no less inspiring, are the stories of the guys we meet every day. Through each man's individual trials, we gain new insight. Unfortunately, some of the best personal testimonies I have ever heard cannot be printed on these pages. In the spirit of total openness and honesty, I will illuminate the central, pivotal role that God has been playing in my own life. May I remind you that it is largely uncharacteristic for guys to be so open? Please accept these thoughts in the spirit intended—as episodes that any man can relate to. If in anything that follows you find cause to judge this writer as having lost his mind, or as something worse, feel free to do so. (You may be right about having lost my mind!) But, it is through real events I know best that I keep the story focused in the right direction—toward the power of the Divine One.

God and Health. I was eighteen years old. Already accredited as co-captain and MVP of a championship high school football team, captain of the baseball team, co-moderator of the youth group, and recipient of congressional appointment to West Point, I guess it was hard to maintain a sense of humility. I had excelled in sports all my life, won a lot, lost some, knew the difference, and preferred winning. Academically, I had above-average grades from a relatively large public high school. I figured college would be demanding, but not overwhelming. All in all, I was a pretty cocky kid.

In the months leading up to my July first report date at the academy, a time fondly referred to as *Beast Barracks*, I did plenty of running, sit-ups, pull-ups, and push-ups, so I could to be ready for the challenge. It worked. Physically, the initial two-month trial was a breeze. Although this phase included a fair amount of mental stress—in particular having to learn so much so fast about how the military operated—almost all the guys managed quite well. Only a few seemed seriously bothered by the continuous barrage of corrections and commands, the incessant testing of newly learned academy trivia, and the frequent employment of hazing techniques against us newcomers. One guy was so unnerved that he decided to thrust himself out of a window. He jumped from the second floor, and he landed on the grass below. No one knew for sure if he was trying to do bodily harm or if he was clever in doing *just enough* to gain his freedom—immediate expulsion.

The start of the school year also meant the beginning of freshman lightweight football practice. I was on a football team where every player was strong and agile. Three other players, I thought, could jump in and do what I was doing. In addition to my growing discouraged on the field, I was shocked at some of my low grades which had been posted on the walls in the academic buildings. It was customary to post all of our grades in all classes—everybody's. In addition to the monthly posting and updating of our grades, the system prescribed our seating arrangement within the class. We sat in order, according to our current grade point average—through three decimals—in that class. Every class was structured the same way. In only a few short months after high school graduation, this pretty smart guy proved to be average or below average in his classes—not exactly an ego booster.

To compound my feeling of utter concern about making it through the first year, not to mention all four, I had broken the cardinal rule of athletics. I dogged it through practice one day, thinking only about having fun on a trip I was supposed to take that weekend. When my fake into the line didn't fool the defense, my naked reverse to the right ended abruptly when I was cut down at the knees from the left. Even the coaches on the sidelines heard the pop of my left knee as it buckled to the turf. Within an hour, the reality of what had just happened began to sink in. Mister physically fit wasn't so cocky any more. The knee was all but shattered; so was my confidence.

From there it was a week of traction to reduce the swelling followed by surgery and six weeks in a full-leg cast. Then came months of rehab which ended just in time for the start of baseball season. It didn't take long to figure out that I had no lateral stability in the knee. My inability to execute the side-to-side pick up drills at spring ball resulted in surgery again, more rehab, and a fitting session for a custom-made, Joe Namath style knee brace.

So far, this was not exactly the college experience I had envisioned. Physical limitations were foreign to me, and I fought them hard. The following year I made up one of the required courses—boxing. But I never really got back to even eighty percent of my former strength or stamina in the legs.

After lots of personal pity parties and hundreds of talks with God, I finally came to the conclusion that I had better focus on completing the academic work as best I could. My physical challenges were not considered critical enough for dismissal. But a failing grade in even one class was as final as a sudden-death playoff. I suppose failing out of a good school is no cause for shame; it is no great honor either. The dropout option held no great appeal.

Through these circumstances, God had served me a generous helping of humble pie. To this day, I know that He also steered me in another direction—toward gaining greater confidence through education. In an environment like West Point, I was never mistaken for a person of academic prowess. What I did have was the inner strength to never quit, never give up, and earn the degree. I am eternally grateful for the opportunity to attend, for all the subsequent blessings that stemmed from my successful completion of the program there, and for the divine guidance and lessons it produced. None of this was evident at the time; the hidden blessing was completely invisible while I was in the recovery room or working my quads in the weight room.

God and Family. I think this one is as tough as they get. Especially when, after twelve years of marriage and two children, two people can't find enough common ground to keep the family unit together. There is just no way to capture all the feelings and emotions that this chapter in my life contained. While I do not intend to withdraw from my emphasis on total candor, I have kept my description of this particular period relatively short; several details simply must remain private.

Where was God when two people decided to divorce? The short answer to this question has a lot to do with the lack of a God-centered relationship between my ex-wife and me, which I described earlier. It was *us*—not Him.

As you might have guessed, divorce provided yet another huge dose of humility. I mentioned earlier how my former spouse and I had become self-assured as young parents. We were blessed by so much—our involvement with church and the kids' school, family support, friends, a good job, decent pay, a nice house and neighborhood, fun times, and some great vacations. Through my ex-wife's parents, we were privileged to participate in some of the upper-crust social events around town. Their business success enabled us all to enjoy some fun trips and occasional appearances at the country club. The combined effect of our comfortable surroundings was our subconscious sense of financial well-being.

After so many years now, I can't tell you how it all went down hill. What I do know is that we were both young and immature at marriage, and I know I did not grow out of that phase very quickly. We did not show each other the love and respect that is needed to maintain a wholesome family environment. So, we chose not to continue in a failing relationship. I cried—a lot—sometimes from emptiness, other times from feelings of guilt or shame. Any number of lonely, despondent, angry, embittered, or totally confused periods all seemed to happen at random within the space of any given week. Some days it seemed as though all such thoughts raced endlessly through my head.

So, where was God? The simple truth is, He couldn't help me until I let Him. About three months after I moved into that first little condo a few miles from the kids, I felt I was going to lose it. I have already described my burning the candle at both ends and being fortunate enough to get back onto the right road, that is, to the local church.

But let's be honest. Don't think for a minute that things just turned around within a few weeks or months. They didn't. It took years of prayer and reflection, years of interaction with others having similar experiences, years of asking for God's forgiveness and believing He would do so, and most of all, years of finding forgiveness for me. Finding my spiritual center, finding my moral compass again, and rediscovering the feeling of being loved, was a process that could only happen by my faith and through His help. It took faith to know God would carry me through in spite of my faults and bad choices.

Funny how easy I find it now to express the concerns that dominated my prayers during those years. My daughters were coming into the most trying years of their lives, yet I was not living with them on a daily basis. Even without having to deal with divorced parents, teenagers and young raging hormones are a wicked combination. The girls became adept at creating new ways to test their boundaries. The normal chaos and anarchy associated with rearing two little blondies was only exacerbated in divorce. For a full ten years, I prayed that we would one day be able to rekindle our relationship—them as my daughters, me as their Dad. Through their early teenage years, they had been exposed to more tension, anger, open hostility, and bad examples than I could imagine. They adopted a confrontational tone with me regularly—way beyond the normal level that teenagers unleash on their parents. But I somehow knew that some day we would regain the love that was being challenged back then. I prayed everyday for our relationship and for our healing. I longed for their forgiveness. God delivered, as only He can.

While God has so richly blessed my family, He has also guided me in terms of where and when I would do something to give back. Let me share more of what God has done.

God and Community. In service within the community or in a non-profit organization, I find that a very simple law applies. It is this: You always *get* more than you *give*. You get more than you give. The pastor of my home church makes the point this way: You can give without loving, but you can't love without giving. I don't know where it started exactly. But for me some form of service has always seemed important. I have been blessed through exposure to many needs—opportunities for service. Maybe you have been, too. Do you enjoy good health, love, friends, food, clothing, shelter, medical care, or a relatively comfortable life style? Do you realize how many people have *none* of these?

As I reflect on various times in my work life and on different groups I've worked with, a few stand out. God had a lesson in mind for me in each one.

- Jaycees. We lived in Peters Township, south of Pittsburgh. The average age of the Jaycees men was thirty or so—a much younger, less structured and business-like organization than the Boy's Club Board I had served on two years prior. I was just one young buck among many who had something to contribute. To this day, I understand why God put me into the Jaycees path. This was where I had been immediately plugged in to the ongoing activities of the group. By becoming an active participant and board member, I regained a genuine sense of joy in giving. It gave me a new awareness of fellowship in working with other men who were equally committed.

- Church: The Board of Deacons. When you spend any amount of time visiting with the sick or shut-ins, with taping a service of worship for their listening pleasure, with parking cars before church, or with working in a small group of caring people, you grow in your own awareness of the many needs of others. And you grow spiritually. Here, I found out that meetings were not super-structured like business meetings; nor were they ever boring or filled with the subtle tensions that so many corporate meetings can have. Thank God I was shown the difference.

- Church: Elder. When you're asked to be a spiritual leader and a role model for other Christians, you have to stop and ask how you could ever feel *qualified* to do either. Fortunately, such service stems from a feeling of being *called* into it rather than a referendum on my personal character traits. Serving as an Elder has been a powerful, rewarding, and humbling experience for me. Emotionally, when other Elders welcome you by the laying of hands, it has profound impact—seemingly right into your soul. This calling (my perception that God is leading me into this work) to our local church's governing body provided plenty of new learning. To a great extent, because of a new rash of social challenges as to what Christian's should believe in order to get up to speed with the modern culture and lifestyles, my service on this board took on even deeper significance. It tested my faith, and, on occasion, changed my perspective. I am convinced that a man never really knows who he is until he takes a stand—verbally and otherwise—and until he forms his own conclusions concerning key issues. I thank God for the experience and all it has meant for me in every aspect of my daily living—not just around the church, but in every group I devote time to.

Being an Elder revealed another unique lesson. In the Presbyterian Church, a person serves for three years actively, and he or she remains an elder from then on. This experience has only deepened my personal commitment to continually discovering God, and to some degree, my sense of responsibility for showing God's love wherever and whenever I can. When this three-year period of active service came to an end, the next opportunity was right around the corner.

When coming off active board services, I was asked if I would help organize a contemporary service—one consisting of more upbeat (code for *younger*) Christian music, and where the service is reverent but absolutely casual and more relaxed than our Sunday services. After six months of checking out other churches' programs and three months of detailed planning for our own, we got started. It was both rewarding and spiritually powerful to see how God had enabled this service to help in some small way to bring others closer to Him.

- Vetshouse, Inc. Before moving away from eastern Pennsylvania, I had a few chances to help out with the Red Cross Homeless Shelter. Time at the shelter was so rewarding that I looked for a similar program in my new hometown. Although a few such shelters existed, I was drawn—*led by God*—to a small group of four or five people who were trying to focus on helping homeless veterans work their way back to productive living. Within six months, we qualified for 501(c) status as a non-profit organization. Then we bought a couple of HUD houses for a dollar each. Through lots of favors and endless donations of time and materials, we renovated the houses, recruited some additional volunteer help, and formed a board. Small as it was then, Vetshouse Inc had a wonderful purpose and mission—helping those who served our country and defended our freedoms. Even with all of its shortcomings, our form of government, I believe, is still the best I have ever seen. It has stood the ultimate test—the test of time.

- Mentoring. Being a big brother for a young teenage boy whose father was deceased has been a personal joy. We seem to have established a relationship where he feels safe in sharing a lot of his inner feelings and emotions. Once again, our relationship had to evolve over time. He did not show an immediate willingness to expose some of his own vulnerabilities. This type of rapport came from my being willing to just listen and not trying to lecture, fix things, or even recommend how he should react in certain situations. I know what you're saying to yourself right now—something like: No way that I could ever relate to a young man like that without doing all those things—especially telling him exactly what he should do or how he should react in his tough situations. I admit it is often tempting to do so.

Here is one little example of the gifts that our time together has given me: By being more of a listener to him, I have become a better listener in other relationships and associations as well—better at home and better at my place of business.

Let me point out one more significant aspect to working with young people. In this case, it has to do with serving as an advisor. It goes back to a couple years prior to my meeting this young man, when I volunteered to help out as a leader for our church senior high youth group. I had always thought of this time with them as a form of prayer. My prayer was simply this: Dear God, as I do all I can to nurture those young adults, please make sure that my two daughters also receive this kind of regular nurturing, since I am not there everyday to be their Dad. I can visualize clergymen cringing right about now. This must really come across as if I were pushing God pretty hard! Make no mistake; this was never an attempt to bargain with God. He doesn't work that way. Nor can any of us ever do enough—churchy things or otherwise—that we earn God's protection for ourselves and for our families. The absolute beauty of the God I believe in is that my blessings have come from His Grace.

So I thank God every day that I can be of some good to others—to my daughters, to my young friend, to my peers, to my extended family, and to strangers in the course of daily encounters.

- JDRF. This stands for the Juvenile Diabetes Research Foundation. Several years ago, a couple of women came into my place of business. They worked for JDRF. I supported their annual walkathon fund raisers, their flea markets, and a few of their annual gala fundraisers. I was drawn to JDRF because of my wife's Type I diabetes which altered her life radically at the tender age of thirteen. Also, our nephew was diagnosed as Type I at an even younger age, and he has touched our hearts. Such a big man at age six or seven when he first learned how to give himself shots, and he learned to monitor his own blood sugar levels. I sincerely hope to see a cure for this life-altering, sometimes life-threatening disease within my lifetime. So I continue contributing in some way to groups which are focused on this goal.

Allow me one final point about JDRF. I don't know exactly where God is when it comes to major diseases or illnesses—especially among children. Diabetes is a classic example, although it is not necessarily fatal as in the case of leukemia or cancer. I have witnessed inspirational times when the inner resilience of a child has become a spiritual foundation and source of strength for his parents, friends, and others who know him well. The strong spiritual bond that such families have formed may in fact be part of the ultimate message. Having little or no comprehension of how God works in these circumstances, we simply have to trust that God has a plan.

If we could sit together for a while, we could name any number of diseases or situations that have a similar impact on family lives. The main point, I think, is this: If we have faith in God and trust in Him, then we cling to the belief that there is something to be gained and learned through every situation we find ourselves in. Health issues are no exception.

Belief in and trust in God are the very *essence* of what my parents, grandparents, several church leaders, teachers and coaches along the way have helped me understand. None of my trust in God is coincidental. It is anything but. Do you think God hasn't figured all this out already? Notice the chapter and verse which occupies the very center position in the Bible. Here's a hint: Psalm 117 is the shortest chapter in the whole Bible, and Psalm 119 is the longest. Each of these, in fact, has a lot to say about faith and trust in God.

Psalm 118 is the central chapter. The verse that is found midway through this psalm, and therefore rests in the very middle of the whole Bible, reads: "It is better to take refuge in the Lord than to trust in man." (Psalm 118, verse 8). Let me assure you that taking refuge has nothing to do with passivity, weakness, or any form of withdrawal from the challenges of daily life. It is about our obedience to God's commandments and our trust in His guiding hand.

Allow me to share one other personal observation with you. As we look back over our toughest personal trials, we most often find that they became sources of personal growth—professionally, spiritually, medically, or otherwise. The old cliché that rocks are what we use to climb on is actually true. As young kids and as adolescents we learned something about competing—sometimes winning, sometimes not. But in any case the crucial learning point for us was to never quit. As young adults—heck, as adults period—we are at a new level, a more critical stage, where we compete in new and different ways and the stakes are higher. We apply our own sense of judgment, our own values, and our own sense of right and wrong. Guys, I believe it is the rules we choose to play by, not the results, which make all the difference. I guarantee you that the children we influence have extraordinarily keen senses about such things. They observe us and absorb our traits like sponges. Think of what they are getting from us now.

If the dominant theme of my messages throughout this work has any appeal to men, the core concept is about the *values* that we men portray. Perhaps the best summary I have ever read on the subject is from a book called *The Craft of Christian Teaching*, by Israel Galindo. He offers a concise version of a larger work by Raths, Harmin and Simon, entitled *Values and Teaching: Working With Values in the Classroom*. Rather than going into it in full detail here, I have included a personal summary from this book in the Appendix. We all have our own sense of values, and we know which ones we hold as non-negotiables. We have a sense of where our integrity comes from. I believe the summary may shed some light on how we form our values and how they become ingrained in us. Understanding this process can help us ensure that the younger lives we touch embrace the ideals we desire for them.

While it bears repeating that these pages are about men's values, it also presents the straight-forward question of how well we live by them. Somewhere along the way, we figure out that it is necessary to control our emotions. At certain times we all feel like we have really messed up in our handling of some tough situation or other. We must back away from these inner doubts occasionally. We can take great comfort in knowing that we are human, that sometimes we flat-out blow it, and that we will figure out how to grow through this particular circumstance, too.

As we have been looking back at the points on our star, this time from the perspective of seeing God's influence in each area, let's also take another glimpse at our work lives.

God and Work. Answer a couple of easy questions for yourself.

Question 1: Where do we spend the majority of our waking hours?
[Answer: At work.]

Question 2: Do you think our faith and our belief in God stops at the door of our workplace?
[Answer: No, but we may act as though it does.]

So how does our faith show up in our workplace? Well, let's go back and take a look at some of the events you read about earlier. Look especially at what happens when things do not necessarily go our way. Men often think it is part of our genetic make-up to view work problems as potentially devastating events; such thoughts are understandable—and usually wrong.

The business, work-a-day world judges us by our performance. That much is true. A man may also be judged by the title he holds, by his position, by his income level, or by where he buys his work clothes. My response: Do the work, and damn the judges. Judge yourself. Hold firmly to what you value and who you are. This does not mean that we can stop learning and shaping what we believe. By interacting with others at work, and by being challenged on our core beliefs, we end up fine-tuning ourselves and hopefully evolving into a person with even greater perspective and personal depth. So, challenges are looming? Bring 'em on!

Let me turn back to my first real job. As the program went, college graduation included a commission as a junior officer and a career. Within a month or so, I had a diploma, a commission, a job, and a wife. Even though I chose not to stay in the service after the initial five year commitment, I was blessed by the opportunity to serve our country. I counted it a huge blessing to win the appointment to the academy. Still, in the constant awareness of how much it meant to me to serve in those years to the best of my ability, I received a much unexpected message as I was preparing to resign my commission. I had announced that I was heading off to a new position with the local division of a large corporation. A certain colonel above me pulled me aside. When I described my new job plans, all he said was, "I envy you."

His brief words were surprising to me. Two other colonels and one general had already asked me to stop and reconsider, which meant that they really thought I should stay in. But those three little words from the colonel gave me a huge surge of confidence. It was a message from out of the blue. What it said to me was, "It's going to be okay; you will be successful in your new venture. *Go for it!*" Only in retrospect did I understand that it was God's way of speaking to me through that man's counsel.

I've already described to you one of my toughest situations—my work with the relatively large British-based firm. Though it was an emotional struggle, especially to be sure that my resigning wasn't just quitting, it was easy to walk away from once I made the decision. To have stayed on, albeit in a lesser role, would have meant denying my own core values. Amazingly, and beautifully, this happened at a time when I was truly focused on doing God's work within my church. I am convinced it was this focus which sustained me. I cannot adequately describe the lack of inner tension or the feeling of *freedom* which stemmed from understanding God's presence in such a scenario. But, it served as proof positive what was written long ago, "… seek first His kingdom, and His righteousness, and all these things will be given to you as well" (Matthew 6, verse 33).

An equally powerful verse in the Bible goes like this: "If God is for us, who can [ever] be against us" (Romans 8, verse 31)? Just in case I had forgotten that message, my understanding and beliefs were put to the test again five years later. I was let go—restructured, if you think that sounds better. But no matter what you call it, it is still a potential threat to a man's livelihood. And it's no fun. The words *you are being terminated* have a nasty ring to them, especially when in the previous three years I had enjoyed every day on the job. I had received promotions along the way. My employer acquired another company of similar size which meant constant change and an opportunity to take on greater responsibilities. This period was enjoyable, that is, until our senior executive group was overhauled. While driving the new team to change the culture of our old, established company, the new president saw an opportunity to consolidate the management force—a polite way of saying *save money*—by firing me and spreading my areas of responsibility to other managers.

Fortunately, there had been enough hints about impending changes months before he acted. In part from exposure to corporate behavior, but to a larger extent through Divine Providence, I was able to handle the situation well. I promise you God had a hand in the way this went down. I want to recap the event for you, largely because of the amusement value I found in it afterwards. It is, in fact, a testimonial as to how well God can carry a man through a tough time.

On a Thursday afternoon, the Vice President called me to say he was coming to see me on Monday, just to talk. Now, that alone was strange; he had never offered to visit me in the nine months he had been with the company. I called the Vice President of Human Resources—a man I knew to be very classy and honorable—to ask what was really going on. While he never offered a specific answer, his tone and his pause communicated plenty. We both knew full well what was going down. Still on Thursday and only minutes later, I received another call from the boss to say he would be flying in by 11:00 am the next day. And, by the way, the visit was for him to pick up the company car and drive it back to the corporate offices. He would also appreciate it if I could have the car packed and ready with all of the company's property such as laptop, stationary, monitor, and keyboard—things I would no longer need since I was being terminated.

Where was God in that episode? A few days prior to this visit, I had reserved a van for a week starting that particular Saturday. My mother-in-law and sisters-in-law were coming for a visit. We had some tours of Colonial Williamsburg and a few other fun stops all lined up. For me, it turned into a perfect opportunity to back away from the work situation, relax some, and let time help put what had just happened into perspective. This actually became a six to eight month process of re-creating my career, but the beginning point—that first week—was *Divinely timed*. I would never want to make light of the fact that I was feeling hurt, unappreciated, a loser, and rejected. Even though I could see it coming and I was in the process of making my next career move, it doesn't change the empty, hollow feeling of getting canned. Nor would I want to ignore the fact that God's hand was in it step for step. I think God was very testy with me during the ensuing months, even to the proverbial eleventh hour. I landed the new position with only one week left of my severance package. For a guy with a new house, new mortgage, new car, child support, higher health care costs, and a local tax increase, one week seemed to be cutting it too close. I think I aged five years that last month.

I can recall bouncing back and forth for three months, between worry and doubt and back to spiritual confidence again. This time of introspection proved once again that faith is a man's powerful ally. This period produced in me a more solid foundation—confidence and trust in God—more so than ever before. Several years earlier I learned that I could be content living with all of the modern creature comforts, or living without them. I had experienced both. In truth, neither status defined who I was or what I believed.

Are you among the hundreds of people, maybe thousands, who trust only in what they have in their bank accounts and 401(k)'s? Now don't go misinterpreting the question. Money isn't wrong or bad—not at all. But basing our personal confidence only in our material wealth is a dead end road. Doing as God instructs and having genuine faith in Him, this is where we find riches like we've never dreamed of. I want to encourage you to pursue the freedom mentioned a while back—freedom that comes from *trusting in Him.*

If I believed that God was guiding me in any of these other aspects of my life, I could never deny His role in my deepest personal relationships. I've given you plenty of insight into my first marriage which ended in divorce. All I would like to share now is something about God within this idea of having a soul-mate.

God and Love. I really did think that a special person would enter into my world when I moved to Virginia. Exactly one month before my move back to my condominium in Pennsylvania, ready to start up the manufacturers' rep business, this very person appeared on the scene. Was that God's way of testing me until the eleventh hour again? By moving back there on a full time basis, I would be closer to my daughters. A good buddy of mine and I often enjoyed coffee and conversations on the back deck of my place in Virginia. I recall describing to him one morning my idea of the perfect woman. (Forget the ones that just popped into your head!) I felt she had to be good looking, physically fit, preferably athletic, smart, and at least believing in God if not possessing a solid religious background. See what a little life experience does? My criteria would have looked significantly different three years prior. A few months following that conversation, a single gal moved in with another single woman in the neighborhood. She lived next door. It turns out this new arrival was only staying for six months, pending a school she was to attend in Richmond. Shortly after I shuffled my primary belongings back to Pennsylvania, this new person of interest and I got together a few times. I asked her to come up and visit. She wanted to and did. Who knew she would meet the mental criteria I had thought to be important? It seems I met hers, too.

We had not become infatuated with each other. A unique bond grew slowly over the next three to six months. And I remember one particular conversation which confirmed my feeling that this lady was special. Coming home from work one evening, I found a note stuck in my front door—from my new lady friend. It was very short and very personal. It was about her personal health issues. Her brief conclusion was that having revealed these things she would understand if I chose to stop seeing her. I recognized in an instant how open, honest, down-to-earth, and loving that was for her to do. I absolutely wanted to learn more about this person who displayed such a strong sense of openness, vulnerability, trust, and honesty. She knew herself well, and she made no bones about speaking in direct and candid terms. How refreshing!

Our mutual respect soared from that point forward. And months later I came to appreciate another interesting fact from her old life experience. She swore never to live "up North" again. So, you guessed it, she moved to Pennsylvania; and we married.

We enjoy a relationship now such as I hope every man comes to know with a soul mate. We are both convinced, even more so with each passing anniversary, that God put us together. She has shown me what love really is and is all about. Can a woman drive a man crazy? Yes, in more ways than one. Can a woman's rationale often escape all logic? Definitely. That is how many women are built. Can a woman make a man feel he rules the world? She absolutely can, if he is lucky enough to have found a true partner.

Being forever candid, then, let me reaffirm that marriage is not a utopian world. We kid a lot about this one: I knew I found Miss Right, but I didn't know at the time that her first name was Always! Seriously, and please watch this closely, with all that our relationship has become, the real focal point of our relationship is our faith and belief in God. As so many of these stories illustrate, it is a man's faith in God which affects every area of his life—not the other way around.

Can you understand now why I believe God needs to be in the center of our star? Whether we recognize it or not, He is in our daily life—with our spouse, in our family, at work, in our community, in health issues, and in nature.

If men put God first, and if we allow God to act in our lives, we will come to know first-hand what genuine happiness and joy are all about.

As I look back and examine the times that were defining moments—work challenges, relationship issues, divorce, or knee surgeries—I realize that God was guiding me. Sometimes the emerging message felt like a form of punishment or discipline. Yet, at other times the message was one of encouragement and reassurance. The key is this: I never would have received all the messages and learned from them if not for two critical behavioral changes on my part. And, here they are for your consideration:

- First, being open to hearing God's voice and seeking to understand His intentions, whatever circumstances we are in. In his letter to the Philippians, the Apostle Paul said it best, "… for I have learned to be content whatever the circumstances" (Philippians 4, verse 11). The same verse paraphrased: I have learned that I can live healthy or ill, rich or poor, and be able to find the good in either. We rarely learn this secret of happiness until we are centered in God.

- Second, making time for quiet reflection—personal time—where you just sit or lay down and listen to the thoughts and feelings that enter your mind. I believe this is extremely important. This is why the first hour or so of my morning belongs to God. These days, I have found no substitute for my morning quiet time on the back deck or on the dock.

Time *with* and *in* the Bible is essential. As I have indicated more than once, it is truly amazing how often a random Scripture reading addresses a particular issue that I may be thinking about or struggling with. I am fully confident that such times are no coincidence. And this same thought introduces another aspect of God's nature: He sends us messages all the time. We only need to believe, and listen.

I believe the Bible is the only real how-to book of its kind. Abraham Lincoln once referred to the Bible as the best and most up-to-date book of all time. In it, you will hear God's voice. I believe that if you truly quiet yourself, you may even hear the whispers of some of the saints that have gone before you—your grandfather, your uncle, your father, or an old friend. The saints recorded in the Bible—men such as Abraham, Noah, Jacob, Joseph, Moses, and Paul—are revealed to us for our instruction and guidance. What each man had in common was an intense love for his God and an unshakable commitment to being obedient to Him.

In the opening chapter, I presented the star as a visual reminder of the key areas of our lives. In the center was God Himself. By now, I trust you have seen a glimpse of God's hand and His influence in these major aspects. I believe our greatest strength is found in our personal relationship with Him.

If you are willing to look to God for daily guidance, you will find Him. And He will sustain you. Our Lord Jesus wraps it up this way,

"Ask and it will be given to you; seek and you will find; knock and the door will be opened to you. For everyone who asks receives; he who seeks finds; and to him who knocks, the door will be opened" (Matthew 7, verse 7).

Indeed.

Epilogue

It shouldn't surprise you that what has been written here represents just a fraction of the dialogues that guys can have with one another. Let me say to you plainly that these types of conversations are happening all over the country—guys meeting with other guys—listening to each other, venting whenever they feel the need, talking candidly without threat or judgment from the others. There is nothing like having a band of brothers who hold one another accountable.

The inherent risk in writing about so many personal things as I have may be become obvious to you. For one thing, time has a way of clouding how past events are viewed. Minor details of what I have recalled may be slightly different from the reality, but such minutiae have no bearing on the messages. I stand behind the descriptions as written.

Let's also be clear that these various points on my wheel and my star are just that—*my* points. I find it extremely important that we recognize when love is present, and understand the impact on us when it is not. We men have an obligation to provide for our families, and the support we provide extends far beyond the material things. So much of our time is invested in our work places; after all, we see ourselves as breadwinners. Our constant challenge is to ensure we are as diligent at home as we are at work. Keeping our priorities in focus, I submit that our service within the community is another worthy aspect of our active lives. When guys are so consumed with roles and responsibilities, it becomes imperative that we also take time to tend to our personal health. Whenever possible, I contend that we should include time communing with Mother Nature.

Finally, we men have an internal need to discover and strive toward our individual purpose. In all that we do, who or what is it all for? In addressing such a personal question, I would encourage you to consider where you have placed God. I believe that it is only when we work toward building our world as He intends, and when we turn to Him for strength and support, that we find a sense of meaning in all of our busyness. These and other aspects that you feel are the most significant are simply a means to check ourselves. We can use the star image over and over again to ensure that we are staying the course that we ourselves have authored. With a plan in place, we can then work harder at creating balance among the elements. We will then find ourselves happier and more content, knowing we are following our priorities just as we would a road map. Whether in the course of a day or two—but certainly within each week—we will know that we have achieved both balance and personal peace.

What all of us share is the fact that our next chapters are already unfolding, even as we do the work and serve in the roles we have been committed to thus far. For instance, I now have a beautiful little grandson to nurture, instruct, and generally have a lot of fun with. While my professional life continues to run its course, I am finding that God has other uses for me. In obedience to His calling, I am working more closely than ever before within my church and in its men's groups. I have held memberships in country clubs. But I cannot think of a better club to belong to than the faith-based groups I serve now.

In any case, these are my genuine thoughts. If any portion of this work can be used to help just one man grow, I consider my writing as having been worth every minute. My personal prayer is that more of us men—men of faith—wake up to the omnipresent needs around us. Even while so many men are already fully engaged in this process, how grand it will be when the Judeo-Christian values that these United States were founded upon are duly recognized and returned to their rightful place.

In plain language, the next step is up to you.

How To Recognize A Star Man

He:

- Will look people in the eyes when talking to them.
- Will regularly show compassion or empathy toward others—the elderly, the impoverished, the wounded, the young, the sick, the physically or mentally handicapped, the friend or relative in need, the homeless, the lonely, the down-trodden, or the suffering.
- Can verbalize his feelings and emotions with someone he trusts.
- Will speak and act (both privately and publicly) in ways that build up and support his spouse—never-never-never in ways that tear her down or offend her spirit.
- Keeps confidences.
- Makes a genuine attempt to look for the good in others.
- Smiles with genuine warmth and sincerity; smiles with his eyes, too.
- Sings, whether he can carry a tune or not.
- Knows the difference between intimacy and sex and would not dream of forcing either.
- Listens. Really listens.
- Makes an equal effort to understand others and be understood by others.
- Believes in God as the Supreme Being, higher authority, and source of strength and inner peace.
- Chooses to obey the laws where he lives or works to reform them.
- Controls his anger and channels it for good within a proper frame of mind.
- Will never physically or mentally abuse his spouse or his family. Such conduct is never acceptable. No exceptions.

- Treats his mate with respect and caring.
- Has goals and can describe them in two minutes.
- Takes care of himself in all respects—medically, mentally, and physically.
- Cares enough about some needs within the community to be an active part of serving them.
- Is all these things or does these things whether or not anyone is watching.
- Enjoys and appreciates Mother Nature—her beauty, and her splendor.
- Is not caught up in the pursuit of material wealth and money. Neither is his sole focus.
- Takes time for himself each day, if for only a few minutes, to quiet himself and stay centered.

Food For Thought and Discussion

Concerning:

Love

1. Have I known the love of a soul mate?
2. Am I giving and receiving in a loving relationship now?
3. Does the woman in my life *know* that she is loved? How and how often do I reinforce this message?
4. What "little things" can I do this week that my mate will appreciate?
5. How well do I communicate with my mate through a simple look or touch?

Family

1. What are the best things I remember about my family: As a child? As a teenager? As an adult?
2. How has my family background had an impact on my life today?
3. If I could change one thing in my family life today, I would: _____.
4. The most important things I want my family to learn or understand from me are: _____.

Work

1. In my work life, what I am trying to accomplish is:
   _____.
2. Am I truly happy in my present role or position?
3. If not, I am prepared to change this situation by (action steps):
   _____.
4. Being honest with myself, the personal traits which I want to change are:
   _____.
5. The core values which guide me every day are:
   _____.
6. Have I rationalized my constant focus on work at the expense of other priorities?
7. If so, what I am willing to do to fix it is:
   _____.

Community

1. Some community groups or civic activities that interest me are:
   _____.
2. What I do (or can do) to give back to my community is:
   _____.
3. The reason(s) I would like to become more involved in this is (are):
   _____.
4. I will start by: (doing what) _____, (when) _____.

Health

1. My physical regimen for staying healthy includes:
   Exercise Habits—
   Eating Habits—

Vitamin Supplements—
For Mental Health—

2. My best times for exercise are:
   _____.

3. Areas I need to work on are:
   _____.

4. Someone I could do this together with is:
   _____.

5. To enjoy Mother Nature, what I like to do is:
   _____.

God

1. Of all the points on the star, I feel my strongest areas are:
   _____.

2. My weakest areas are:
   _____.

3. The way I can move toward a condition of better balance is:
   _____.

4. Some ways that I can make sure I am staying focused on God include:
   _____.

5. Having thought about all the points on the star, I would revise it a little bit. I see my own key points as being (sketch your own star points):

Notes

For more information about the author, please address correspondence to:

1312 Rylands Road
Virginia Beach, VA 23455

Email: gcombs1@cox.net

Appendix

The following text is taken from the work of Raths, Harmin and Simon, entitled "*Values and Teaching: Working With Values* in the Classroom." The excerpt below provides a more condensed summary of the original text, as created by Israel Galindo in his work titled "*The Craft of Christian Teaching*." It is helpful to understand the way values become ingrained in us, and it provides us Dads with some tools to help us raise our children. May I also suggest reading beyond these selected pages since the book offers insightful tips on how to *teach* values as well?

In a few places, I have replaced the word "Christian" with the words Judeo-Christian." This is intentional. For I believe there is a richness in our heritage that extends back to the days of our Jewish roots. I believe the term is more inclusive, and helps us recognize and respect this fact.

Also note that where the original authors have used the word "learners," I would suggest we substitute the words children, siblings, other loved ones, or friends. One or more of these may be more applicable to your specific situation.

How Values Are Formed

As Judeo-Christian teachers, it is important that we understand how a value is formed. Knowing how values are formed will enable us to figure out ways to teach our learners to enable them to choose Judeo-Christian values for living. According to Raths, Harmin, and Simon, the process of valuing develops in the three-step framework of (1) choosing, (2) prizing, and (3) acting. Within this framework, seven components must be present for a value to exist.

Choosing

1. *Choosing freely.* Values must be freely chosen; they cannot be coerced. Learners must have the opportunity to make a choice freely.

2. *Choosing from among alternatives.* Values result only when choices exist; bona fide alternatives must exist from which to choose. Learners must be exposed to legitimate alternatives from which to choose.

3. *Choosing after thoughtful consideration of the consequences of each alternative.* Values do not develop through intuition or guessing; they are formed only after weighing the range of alternatives and their consequences. Learners need to be guided through the hard work of thinking through choices and their consequences.

Prizing

4. *Prizing and cherishing.* A value is a positive part of the person. Values feel good; they make us feel happy to own them. They are cherished because they guide our lives. Learners need to feel positive about the values they choose.

Acting

5. *Affirming.* Values that are freely chosen and with which we are pleased are affirmed; we are willing to publicly share our values. Learners need opportunities to express and publish their values.

6. *Acting upon choices.* When we have formed a value, we "put our money where our mouth is" and we "walk the talk," that is, we give evidence in our living of what we truly value. Ideas, truths, and learning that do not manifest themselves in the way we live are not values. Learners need ways to examine their lives to determine which values are real for them.

7. *Repeating.* Values become patterned in our lives. They become part of our life structure and manifest themselves in several areas of our lives: public and private, recreational and vocational. Learners need opportunities to practice their values in all areas of their lives.

Suggested Further Reading For Men

With so many great works to select from, I find it difficult at best to focus on only a few. I am certain you will enjoy any of these:

The Man in The Mirror—by Patrick Morley

The Man God Uses—by Henry and Tom Blackaby

Half Time—by Robert Buford

Annointed For Business—by Ed Silvoso

Spiritual Leadership—by Henry and Richard Blackaby

If It's Going To Be, It's Up To Me—by Robert H. Schuller

Desiring God—by John Piper

The Purpose Driven Life—by Rick Warren

Soul Feast—by Marjorie J. Thompson

Take A Second Look At Yourself—by John Homer Miller

First Steps To Knowing God's Will—by S. Maxwell Coder

Men Are From Mars, Women Are From Venus: A Practical Guide for Improving Communication and Getting What You Want in Your Relationships—by John Gray

About the Author

Gary W. Combs

Gary Combs currently serves as an Elder in the Presbyterian Church, where he has also been sustained as a Commissioned Lay Pastor. He has been active among men's ministries for over 15 years and is passionate in his commitment to serving others. Gary holds a Bachelor of Science Degree from West Point in 1975, and he took post-graduate courses in business at Rider University. Gary was commissioned into the U. S. Army, where he served five years of active duty.

During his early business career, Gary progressed from technical sales, to product management, and to marketing management for a Fortune 500 company and for an international conglomerate. He founded and operated his own business, a manufacturers' representative agency, from the late eighties into the early nineties.

Gary rejoined corporate life as president of U.S. operations for the foreign-based company he had been representing. Feeling a need for change, he joined a U.S.-owned firm as a product manager then as a general manager. Gary's career is still unfolding, as he is a marketing executive in wholesale distribution.

Throughout his career, Gary has served his church and his community. In addition to his leadership roles within the church, he has applied his energies in such organizations as the Boys' and Girls' Club and the Jaycees. At various times he has spoken at business and community meetings or conferences. Gary has been recognized in the publication of Outstanding Young Men of America, 1982 and 1986, and in the American Registry of Outstanding Professionals, 2005–2006.

Gary and his wife, Joni, live in Virginia Beach, Virginia. He has two daughters, both now living independently, one having completed her bachelor degree and the other in her third year of study toward a degree in education.

978-0-595-41291-4
0-595-41291-2

Printed in the United States
102402LV00003B/214-273/A